Date Due

D1214884

TEACHING ABOUT TECHNOLOGY

Science & Technology Education Library

VOLUME 27

SCOPE

The book series *Science & Technology Education Library* provides a publication forum for scholarship in science and technology education. It aims to publish innovative books which are at the forefront of the field. Monographs as well as collections of papers will be published.

The titles published in this series are listed at the end of this volume.

Teaching about Technology

An Introduction to the Philosophy of Technology for Non-philosophers

by

MARC J. DE VRIES

Eindhoven University, The Netherlands

 Springer

A C.I.P. Catalogue record for this book is available from the Library of Congress.

ISBN-10 1-4020-3409-1 (HB) Springer Dordrecht, Berlin, Heidelberg, New York
ISBN-10 1-4020-3410-5 (e-book) Springer Dordrecht, Berlin, Heidelberg, New York
ISBN-13 978-1-4020-3409-1 (HB) Springer Dordrecht, Berlin, Heidelberg, New York
ISBN-13 978-1-4020-3410-7 (e-book) Springer Dordrecht, Berlin, Heidelberg, New York

Published by Springer,
P.O. Box 17, 3300 AA Dordrecht, The Netherlands.

Printed on acid-free paper

TABLE OF CONTENTS

TABLE OF CONTENTS

PREFACE

Writing this book has been quite a challenge. Philosophy for many people as practical as teachers can be often has a reputation of being unpractical, difficult to understand, dull, and more of those not so positive connotations. Yes, it is my firm belief that teachers, at whichever level of education, could greatly benefit from philosophy. I had this experience myself when I became involved in the development of Technology Education as an example of teaching about technology at the primary and secondary level. It sometimes felt like one was inventing one's own school subject, and I strongly felt the need to search for a sound conceptual basis for that. Writings about the philosophy of technology helped be enormously to build up this basis for myself and communicate it to others. Whenever one wants to teach about something, it is necessary to be clear about what it is that one teaches about. Philosophers are concerned in particular with questions like that, for example: what is this 'thing' called 'technology'. Thus I became connected to the philosophy of technology, and later on even moved into this field fulltime. Still today I use the many opportunities to link philosophy and educational issues in my daily work. When having finished a philosophical study, I immediately start asking myself: what does this mean for teaching about technology? And most of the times I find that this teaching can be improved by taking into account those philosophical considerations. With this book I hope I can enable others to have similar experiences. The challenge, though, was to present the philosophy of technology in such a way that is becomes fully accessible to non-philosophers. Those non-philosophers can be teacher educators that teach about technology to future teachers, or those who teach introductory courses about the philosophy of technology to students in engineering, either in colleges or universities. Perhaps the book even appeals to those who already teach about technology at the primary or secondary level. It may help them to become more aware of what it is that they teach about, and hopefully it will help them improve their teaching by means of the insights that philosophy of technology offers.

The title of this book is loosely related to other book titles. Carl Mitcham wrote an introduction into the philosophy of technology for philosophers under the title 'Thinking Through Technology'. Later, Joseph Pitt wrote his book on the philosophy of technology under the title 'Thinking About Technology'. My book is titled 'Teaching About Technology'. To make a full circle someone should write a book titled 'Teaching Through Technology'. That book, however, would not be about Technology Education, but about Educational Technology. As these two terms are often confused, I would like to emphasize here that my book deals with Technology Education, not with Educational Technology (although in one Chapter I pay explicit attention to the use of technology for teaching about technology).

The book ends with an annotated bibliography (Chapter 11), in which readers find the sources that I have used. To give the book a textbook character I have not included notes and references in the various chapters (except for Chapter 7). In most cases it is obvious in which book in the annoted bibliography the various quoted and discussed authors can be found; in cases where this is not obvious there was no source that I found accessible to an audience of non-philosophers, or the source was in a language different from English.

I am grateful to some people who read earlier versions of the text for this book. In particular I want to thank Giacomo Romano and Krist Vaesen, Ph.D. students in our Eindhoven University of Technology philosophy of technology program (at least, that is what they were when they reviewed my draft texts). My thanks go to Lamber Royakkers, my long-term colleague in Eindhoven, who gave some useful advises for the chapter on ethics (Chapter 6). Thanks also to the staff of the technology teacher education program in Marseille, France, led by Jacques Ginestié, for the opportunity of trying out the content of the book in a three day mini-course on the philosophy of technology that I conducted with them in Marseille in July 2004. That was truly a wonderful experience for me. I also want to thank the anonymous reviewer who read my text so carefully and gave some very useful comments.

I want to thank Bill Cobern for his efforts to get the book published as a worthy volume in the book series that is under his editorship. Finally I want to thank Kluwer's Michel Lokhorst, with whom I have now worked for several years on the International Journal of Technology and Design Education, and whom I have learnt to respect greatly, for his role in positioning the book in Kluwer's (now: Springer's) portfolio.

Eindhoven, December 2004   Marc de Vries

Chapter 1

PHILOSOPHY OF TECHNOLOGY: WHAT AND WHY?

What do we mean by 'philosophy' of technology, and why would educators want to know about it? Those are the two questions that will be addressed in this introductory chapter.

The answers to these questions are by no means self-evident. The word 'philosophy' in the first question is used in different ways. A teacher could, for example, state that his or her 'philosophy' in dealing with classes is based on making humans do what they are good at. In that case the word 'philosophy' does not refer to a scientific discipline, but rather to a certain 'approach'. If the word is used in that sense, there is often an interest to get to know this 'philosophy'. If, however, we take 'philosophy' in the sense of a scientific discipline, it is certainly not to be taken for granted that educators would be interested in it. Educators tend to be concerned primarily with day-to-day and down-to-earth types of questions. Why would they take a book like this one other than for personal interests that are not directly related to their teaching profession?

The second question cannot be answered properly without having answered the first one. So let us first consider the meaning of the term 'philosophy' of technology. What is meant by that word in this book?

1.   WHAT IS PHILOSOPHY?

In general philosophy is the scientific discipline that aims at systematic reflection on all aspects of reality. In philosophy we try to gain insight into the real nature of those aspects. We can do this by asking the following question: "what do you mean when you say . . .?" This can be called the *analytical function* of philosophy. Asking such a question can have a practical purpose. It can, for example, help us to get out of dead-ends in debates, in particular when these are caused by naïve use of terms. An example of such a dead-end is the following. For many years people have debated about the issue whether or not technology can be properly called 'applied science'. Such debates were often frustrated because both for the 'technology is applied science' opinion, as well as for the opposite opinion, examples could easily be found. Seemingly there was a paradox: the 'technology is applied science' opinion could be supported by evidence and falsified by evidence at the same time. The example of the transistor could be used as evidence for the 'technology is applied science' claim, but at the same time the steam engine could be used to falsify it. However, the paradox appears to be a fake one only when one asks the question: what did we mean when we said 'science' and what did we mean when we said 'technology' in our debate? It is only then that we start realizing that the paradox is the result of our limited use of the terms. Thanks to that consideration, we are now aware that we have to be careful to make too general claims about science and technology, because there are different types of sciences and different types of technologies. Because we used a particular type of science and technology to support one opinion and a different type of science and technology to support the other opinion, but failed to be explicit about these different uses of the terms, we were not able to reach a consensus. The example illustrates how useful it can be to reflect carefully about what we mean by the words we use. This is where philosophy comes in to help us.

Apart from the analytical function of technology there is a *critical function* of technology. By using the proper language and concepts that were developed by means of the analytical function of philosophy, we can now reflect on things in such a way that we can make value judgments.

Because there are many aspects of reality, there are many 'philosophies'. In this book we will deal with philosophy of technology. That is a relatively young discipline compared to another 'philosophy' that deals with a related aspect of reality, the philosophy of science. In the philosophy of science one deals with questions such as: how does scientific knowledge emerge, what criteria do we use to determine whether or not we are prepared to reckon a certain activity to be 'scientific', what is a scientific theory and how does it relate to reality, what different types of sciences can be distinguished? A third example of a philosophy is the philosophy of mind. This type of philosophy focuses on various aspects of the mental aspect of reality. Some questions that are discussed in the philosophy of mind are: what do we mean by 'intentions', by 'desires', by 'beliefs', what do we mean by 'rationality' and how do intentions, beliefs and desires relate to one another in rational minds? As rationality plays a role in science, there are relations between the philosophy of science and the philosophy of mind. Likewise there are relationships with the philosophy of technology. That is evident when we realize that technology is not only a matter of our hands, but also of our minds. When in philosophy of mind literature we read about general concepts such as 'rationality' of 'agents' that have 'intentions' and 'desires', and by 'reasoning' about 'means-ends relationships', 'plan' their 'actions', these are all concepts that play a role in technology too. Therefore when in later chapters we will study the various aspects of the philosophy of technology, we will come across such concepts again.

Within the discipline of philosophy several fields can be distinguished. Just like in physics we have solid-state physics, nuclear physics, optics, mechanics (classical and quantum), we can also identify different parts of philosophy, each with its own focus. Let us now see what the main fields in philosophy are that we will recognize when a survey of the philosophy of technology is presented in the remaining chapters of this book.

One field in philosophy is *ontology*. It deals with being, with what *is*, what *exists*. A first sight it may seem to be trivial, to ask the question what we mean when we say that something *exists*, and many people will wonder whatever the relevance of asking such a question might be. Yet, there can be situations in which the answer to this question does make a difference. For example, one could ask if technological products really have a systems nature or if this is just something that we have 'invented' to make sense of them. Ontology also asks for the *essence* of things. For example: what makes technology different from nature? When do we call something 'technological' or 'artificial', and when do we call it 'natural'?

Epistemology is a second field in philosophy. It focuses on the nature of knowledge. What, for example, do we mean when we say that we 'know' that the moon circles around the earth? Or what do we mean when we say that we 'know' that the object in front of us is a CD player? In our time, knowledge is seen as an important issue in society. We often speak of a 'knowledge economy', and many people nowadays are interested in what is called 'knowledge management'. What, then, do we mean when we use the term 'knowledge' in those expressions? In education knowledge of course plays a vital role too. For a long time we have consider education to be the transfer of knowledge. Now our view on education is more varied. Knowledge is not always transferred, but sometimes has to 'grow' in individuals. Related to this field is the *philosophy of mind*, in which we reflect on how minds function and can have knowledge and other types of intentions.

In the third place we have *methodology* as a field in philosophy. Here some confusion can easily arise. Methodology is often associated with methods. But that is only part of the truth. The word 'methodology' is composed of three Greek words. 'Metha' means 'through', 'hodos' means 'way' and 'logos' means 'word', but also can have the meaning of 'study'. Literally methodology, or meth-hodo-logy, means: study of (logos) the way (hodos) through which (metha) something happens. When we think of 'methods', such a way is well paved and straightforward. But things do not always come about in such a well-organized manner. Often that way is crooked and rough. Methodology deals with all sorts of ways.

A fourth field in philosophy is *metaphysics*. Metaphysics deals with our visions on reality, and the way we try to make sense of reality. An important issue here is the question of the purposes of our activities. Reflections on purposes are called: *teleology*. This term is not to be confused with 'theology', which is a discipline of its own right. Teleology deals with aims and purposes. For what purpose, for example, do we live, work, play, eat, think, etcetera? The answers to such question are usually closely related to one's worldview. This worldview can be a religion, but it need not be so (hence we should be careful not to confuse teleology and theology). Of course teleology assumes that there are aims and purposes for life. For that reason lots of philosophers consider teleology to be a theory rather than a field of study in philosophy. For non-philosophers, though, the issues that are debated in teleology are probably what they think of in the first place when they hear the word 'philosophy'. It deals with very fundamental questions. For technology it means that we try to understand what drove – and drives – humans to develop and use technologies. Is it just a matter of survival? Or are there other possible motives for behaving like a 'homo technicus'?

In the fifth place, there are *ethics* and *aesthetics* as fields in philosophy. They are taken together here because they both deal with the issue of values. Ethics is concerned with the issue of what is good to be done and what should not be done. Ethics certainly not only deals with specific ethical guidelines, such as those that have been derived from religions. People sometimes think that are shy back from it because they fear for indoctrination. But ethics also deals with logical analyses of ethical dilemmas. *Logic* is a field in philosophy that plays a role in ethics, but also in the other fields in philosophy. It helps people to make proper arguments when reasoning for or against certain decisions with ethical aspects. So ethics is both a field in which specific ethical opinions are discussed, but also provides logical tools for ethical reasoning. Aesthetics deals with values of beauty. What does it mean for something to have beauty? Here logic too plays a role. A popular saying is that beauty can not be argued about. That suggests that reflecting on beauty is just a matter of feelings. But in philosophy it is more and logic can be used to support rational reasoning about beauty no less than about other issues.

All of these fields can be recognized in the philosophy of technology. There is, for example, a growing amount of literature on the 'ontology of technological artifacts'. In that literature philosophers try to get grips on the nature of technological artifacts. When can we say that a certain object *is* a technological artifact? Teleology too features in the philosophy of technology. We can be interested in the question for what different purposes human beings do technology. In this book, chapters 2 through 6 will deal with each of these five fields in the philosophy of technology.

One more way of splitting up the whole field of philosophy into subsections is by dividing this field into analytical and Continental philosophy (Continental because most authors in this strand were German or French, while most of the 'analytical' authors were from the UK or the USA). Although nowadays these two philosophical streams are not as separated as they used to be in the past, and certainly the geographical terms like Continental are now inappropriate, still many contemporary philosophers can be recognized as belonging to one of these two. The difference between the two is roughly that in analytical philosophy the main aim is to conceptualize, and that continental philosophers are more interested in making value judgments about (aspects of) reality. Sometimes the same difference is described as philosophy of language on the one side (because conceptualization to a large extent has to do with the way we use language – words and expressions – to define concepts) and philosophy of culture on the other side (because the value judgments in most cases refer to developments in culture and the role technology has in that). In fact this means that the two functions of philosophy (the analytical and the critical) have been dealt with by separate streams in philosophy. Probably most people get to know the philosophy of technology by reading books in the second strand (the Continental philosophy, or cultural philosophy), because it often appeals more to people to think about social and cultural aspects of technology than to think about how technological concepts can be defined and understood properly. Hopefully the remaining chapters of this book will show that both strands can be equally exciting. And for educational purposes, searching for

clear and well-defined concepts is certainly of no less importance than to
discuss value aspects of technological developments.

So far we have dealt with philosophy in general. Let us now focus on the
philosophy of technology to see the status of that particular field.

2.   WHAT IS PHILOSOPHY OF TECHNOLOGY?

The difference between the continental and analytical traditions is also
found in the philosophy of technology. In the early days of the philosophy of
technology, most authors wrote about the social impacts of technology and
the impacts of society on technology. One could call this way of reflection,
in which the focus is on the relationship between technology and its social
context: 'philosophy *about* technology'. Mitcham uses the term 'humanities
philosophy of technology' for this category. The philosophers we find in this
category often did not have an engineering or natural science background.
Many of them were philosophers 'pur sang'. Perhaps that explains why they
did not reflect so much on what technology is, but rather on the effects it had
on culture and society: they did not have the expertise to make such
reflections. Although this is not necessarily an effect of the humanities
approach, somehow the authors in this category tend to focus on the negative
impacts of technology on society and often warn us to be careful. The
alternative way of reflecting on technology, 'philosophy *of* technology' is
then characterized by the fact that it tries to describe technology itself. Here
we find philosophers of whom several have both a philosophical and an
engineering background. This combination does not occur very frequently,
and perhaps that explains why this second type of reflection of technology
emerged much later and slower than the first-mentioned type. Mitcham uses
the term 'engineering philosophy of technology' for this other category.
Although here too there is no necessary relationship with the engineering
background of the philosophers in this category, these people tend to be
much less critical about technology than their colleagues in the 'humanities
philosophy of technology'. In this strand we also find what is called the
empirical turn in the philosophy of technology. This term indicates the
interest to let one's philosophical agenda be led at least partially by taking
notice of the practice of technology. The idea is that this is helpful in
developing appropriate concepts and ideas in philosophy. It does not turn
philosophy into an empirical science (philosophers still have the freedom to
make statements that have no direct reference to practice) but it does
stimulate philosophers to develop ideas that make sense to practitioners. For
education too, this empirical turn is of interest. In education we like to teach

about technology as we can see it being practiced. A philosophy that has no relationships to that would be less useful for that than a philosophy that has seriously taken into account what happens in practice.

What is also reflected in the philosophy of technology as a general feature of philosophy is the distinction between the fields of ontology, epistemology, methodology, metaphysics (and in that field teleology) and ethics. In his survey of the development of the field of philosophy of technology, titled 'Thinking Through Technology', Carl Mitcham has identified four main approaches. According to him reflections on technology have focused on four ways of conceptualizing technology: as objects, as knowledge, as actions and as volition. In the first way of conceptualizing technology, we find ontological considerations mainly. Philosophers then ask for the essence of technological artifacts. In the second case, technology as knowledge, of course epistemological studies can be expected. In actions as a viewpoint, methodology is the field of philosophy that is addressed, and in the volition approach, the teleological, ethical and aesthetical considerations are found. In this book Mitcham's division will be used to describe philosophy of technology for technology educators. This division roughly matches the division in the fields of philosophy that we have identified. But as we will see, sometimes the discussion of a field in the philosophy of technology in Mitcham's division will have elements of more than one of the fields of philosophy.

Mitcham in his book makes clear that the philosophy of technology is a pretty young discipline, much younger than, for example, the philosophy of science. As a result, many fundamental issues are still debated quite heavily. On the one hand, one can, of course, say that such debate is inherent for philosophy in general, and in the philosophy of science too, there are still very fundamental debates. But on the other hand, the philosophy of technology does not have as clearly crystallized positions in these debates as in the philosophy of science. There are no 'schools' in the philosophy of technology with a well-established tradition as one can find in the philosophy of science, where we have Popperians, Kuhnians, Lakatos-followers, or Feyerabendians. The philosophy of technology is more like a mosaic of many different ideas and suggestions. Yet, there is lot that one can learn from this mosaic. Mosaics anyway do have their charm.

3. WHY WOULD TECHNOLOGY EDUCATORS WANT TO KNOW ABOUT PHILOSOPHY OF TECHNOLOGY?

It is certainly not self-evident that educators would like to know more about philosophy of technology. For many people philosophy in general is regarded as something that does not have a clear usefulness. Even famous people made statements that reflect this attitude. In his book 'Philosophy for dummies', Tom Morris quotes some of these statements. Voltaire ones wrote: "When he who hears doesn't know what he who speaks means, and when he who speaks doesn't know himself what he means – that's philosophy'. The only thing philosophers seem to do is disagree with each other. Or in William James' words: "There is only one thing that a philosopher can be relied on to do, and that is to contradict other philosophers." The results of that can only be negative, according to Jonathan Swift, who wrote: "The various opinions of philosophers have scattered through the world as many plagues of the mind as Pandora's box did those of the body; only with this difference, that they have left no hope at the bottom."

This does not sound very positive about philosophy. Why then would technology educators spend any time on studying philosophy of technology? Is it perhaps what Socrates said: "The unexamined life is not worth living" (again, quoted from Tom Morris)? Or, applied to technology education: "The unexamined technology is not worth teaching"? Wouldn't it be a poor situation if a technology is taught without any kind of reflection, just as a collection of bits and pieces of knowledge and skills? Would not that easily result in a fairly random choice of what is taught and what is not taught? And would that really contribute to what (future) citizens need to live in a technological world?

Let us consider what those who teach about technology could gain from the philosophy of technology. There are at least four reasons for technology educators to get acquainted with this discipline. The philosophy of technology can be a source of inspiration for determining the content of a curriculum, it can yield insights into how to construct teaching and learning situations, it can provide a conceptual basis and proper understanding of technology which can help technology educators respond to unforeseen situations while teaching about technology, it can help to position the teaching of technology among other subjects, and it can help identity the research agenda for educational research in technology education. All of those will be discussed in this section.

Teaching technology can have several aims. It may be because people need specific knowledge and skills to be able to function in an environment in which technology plays an important part. Another aim may be that people acquire a good, balanced perception of what technology is. One could defend the statement that in fact that is a prerequisite for all functioning in a technological world. Developing a good perception of technology can be important in different cases. For future engineers it is important to know what characterizes the field that they will work in, in order for them to be able to think and act consciously and responsibly. But also for those who will never become engineers but will be constantly confronted with technology in their lives, it is important that they are able to make good, well-informed judgments about the way technology should be approached. Either when the teaching of technology takes place as a professional or academic program, or when this teaching is part of the general education of all people, the question that educators are faced with is: what should be the content of teaching that will help the learners to acquire a good perception of technology? In other words: what should be the content of the curriculum? Philosophy of technology can help answering that question as it provides ideas about what are important features of technology that are inherent to a balanced perception of technology.

Once the content of the curriculum has been determined, the next question is: how can we construct situations that will enhance the acquisition of such a balanced perception of technology in learners? Here too, the philosophy of technology can be a useful resource for considerations. Philosophy of technology can, among other things, provide insights into what makes technological knowledge and skills different from other sort of knowledge and skills. These differences may be important for determining how technological knowledge and skills can be taught and learnt. One of the characteristics of technological knowledge, for instance, appears to be its normative component. The philosophy of technology, in particular the epistemology of technology, has shown that technological knowledge often is related to judgments. Part of the knowledge of engineers has to do with the functions of artifacts, and those can be fulfilled well or badly. Another normative aspect in technological knowledge is that some materials are better suited for usage in a particular artifact than others. The normative knowledge about the relationship between the material properties and the functions that need to be fulfilled in the artifact is another example of the normativity in technological knowledge. Scientific knowledge does not have this kind of normativity. There is normativity in science as well, but mainly with respect to the norms for what we accept as scientific knowledge and what not, and not with respect to the objects of the knowledge. One cannot say that an electron is bad or good. As soon as one starts making statements about its suitability do to something, one has already passed the border to technology, because a practical purpose or application is then at stake. This difference between scientific and technological knowledge, no doubt, has its consequences for teaching those different types of knowledge. A good insight into what characterizes the normativity in technological knowledge can help those who teach technology to make sophisticated decisions when setting up educational settings and situations for the teaching and learning of technology. Later on in this book we will see how.

Teaching and learning is always a matter of interaction. Whatever the teacher has prepared for, the learner too has its influence on what is taught. Often it cannot be foreseen what influence this will be. No one can tell beforehand what questions learners will ask as a response to certain content, presented in the educational situation that has been prepared by the teacher. An educator who has no good perception of technology, but entirely relies on a curriculum that has been designed by other, who had such a perception, will soon find himself or herself in problems when learners start to ask questions that are not directly and/or explicitly addressed in the curriculum content. It is simply not possible to help other people acquire a good perception of technology in educational situations when one self does not hold such a perception.

Reflections on the specific features of technology can also help to position the teaching of technology among the teaching of other subjects. Perhaps the most important example of this is the ever-recurring question of how to find a proper relationship between science and technology education as two elements in general education. As we will see in Chapter 4, the development of scientific knowledge and that of technological knowledge have often gone hand in hand. Yet scientific and technological knowledge are different and have distinct characteristics (above the normativity in technological knowledge has already been referred to). This justifies that teaching technology should be separated from teaching science, yet the two should closely co-operate in order to do justice to the relationship between them. There are different options for this to be realized in educational practice. Philosophical insights into technology, and in science, can help to find proper ways of positioning the teaching of technology among the teaching of science and other subjects.

The development of education about technology ideally should be supported by educational research. Alas, this is often not the case.

Sometimes a lack of interest is the cause for that. Technology is considered to be such a practical subject that one feels no need to develop any kind of theory about its teaching, not even through empirical research into what happens in the educational practice. In other cases a lack of funding is the cause of an absence of educational research in the development of technology education. But fortunately there are other situations in which educational research does have function in the development of curricula and teaching practice. If, however, it is unclear what characterizes technology itself, it will be equally unclear what is to be researched in terms of teaching technology. The philosophy of technology here too can serve as a source of inspiration. In this philosophy the use of the concept of systems has been brought forward as an important feature of technology and engineering. For educational research this raises the question of what pre-concepts pupils and students might have about this. Do they have an intuitive sense that a washing machine is a set of co-operating parts that transform a certain input to a certain output through a certain process? Or do the regard it as just a large collection of nuts and bolts? The philosophy of technology has shown the usefulness of regarding the functional and the physical nature of an artifact. Do pupils and students have that kind of understanding already before they enter our classrooms? How would they describe a knife in the first place? As an object that has a sharp part and a blunt part, which are fit together (the physical nature)? Or would they describe it as a means for cutting bread or meat (the functional nature)? Such insights would be useful to have for those who try to teach about those artifacts. Likewise, philosophical reflections on design processes (in design methodology) can help us determine what would be important to get to know about the way pupils and students design in project work.

It is useful to make a remark about my use of the terms 'technology' and 'engineering'. I have abstained from any effort to give a definition of technology. For those who are looking for a definitions: there are thousands out there to choose from and I do not think I can come up with the one that beats them all. Throughout the book I will take the term 'technology' in the broad sense of the human activity that transform the natural environment to make it fit better with human needs, thereby using various kinds of information and knowledge, various kinds of natural (materials, energy) and cultural resources (money, social relationships, etc.). I will take engineering in the same broad sense, only distinguishing it from technology in that engineering is when professionals called 'engineers' do the human activity described above. The term includes not just mechanical and electrical engineers, but also architects and textile designers (in general: all those professionals that develop and make new technological devices, systems and processes). The term 'technology' also includes the users as humans that are involved in this activity. In my description of the philosophy of technology the terms 'technology' and 'engineering' both apply, and I will let my choice between the terms be led by the literature that I refer to in a particular case.

Now that we have a first impression of what philosophy of technology deals with and in what sense it can be useful to educators, we now turn to the various fields of the philosophy of technology in order to get a more in-depth view on the ideas that have been developed so far. We will start with the issue of technological artifacts.

Chapter 2

TECHNOLOGICAL ARTIFACTS

Ask a young child what technology is, and most probably he or she will start listing examples of technical artifacts. That is what several empirical studies among young people have shown (in Chapter 7 we will discuss that in more detail). Technical artifacts are our immediate encounter with technology. We may not see all that much of all the process behind technology, but the outcomes of such processes, artifacts, are everywhere. In this Chapter we will explore how we can distinguish technical artifacts from other objects in our lifeworld, and also how they have their place of that lifeworld and interact with us.

1. NATURAL OBJECTS, INSTRUMENTS, TOOLS AND ARTIFACTS

Suppose someone walks in the forest and picks up a thick bough to lean on. With a bit of fantasy one could call that a very simple example of technology. After all, a human has used an object for a practical purpose. And most people would agree that this is the very heart of what we call technology. But at the same time we would not like to equate the bough with a cane that another stroller in the forest had bought in a shop and took with him when going out for his walk. Although the bough and the cane are now used for the same purpose, they have a different history. The cane once started its life as a bough, but has been modified considerably in order to be able to fulfill its role as a cane. The first stroller's bough did not go through such a process. This difference can be used to distinguish between natural objects and tools. These are terms that were coined by Randall Dipert in a book on artifacts in art and in technology. In his terminology an *instrument* is a natural object that we use for a practical purpose without having modified it. A *tool* then is an object that a human being has *modified* in order to make it suitable for serving a certain practical purpose. Simply said: the first stroller's bough is a natural object, while the second stroller's cane is a tool.

Dipert also defines a third type of object that we can find in technology: an *artifact*. What, then, is the difference between a tool and an artifact? Well, Dipert identifies the possibility that a human being can not only modify an object for serving a practical purpose, but also do that in such a way that the modified object *displays* what it is now meant for. The example that Dipert uses to illustrate this concept is a chair. According to Dipert it is more than a matter of functionality that a chair seems to invite you to sit on it. The designer has deliberately given the chair such a shape that it displays what you are supposed to do with it. Although the example was meant to support the validity of the concept of artifacts in Diperts' terminology, it also can be used to show how problematic Dipert's distinction between tools and artifacts is. It is not very probable that every designer of a chair will pay explicit attention to the issue of how the chair can display its function. But suppose some designers do, while others don't. The consequence would be that chairs from designers that did not pay explicit attention to that should be called 'tools', while artifacts from designers that did pay attention to it should be called 'artifacts'. That is confusing. Also if one would abstain from taking into the account the designers' intentions and only look at the outcome (does the object display its function, intended or not intended) then the problem would be shifted to the user: does he or she think that the object display a certain function? Some will do, others will not. Again there is an ambiguity: for some the chair will be a tool, for others it will be an artifact. This makes clear that the boundary between tools and artifacts in Dipert's terminology is not unproblematic and therefore we will abandon it. From now on we will use the word artifact for any object that has been modified, whether or not it displays what it has been modified for. That means we will combine his concepts of tools and artifacts and call them both artifacts.

2. ARTIFACTS, FUNCTIONS AND PHYSICAL PROPERTIES

The bough and cane in our initial example both serve as a support for the strollers to lean on. To indicate this practical purpose we can use the term *function*. This term is used widely in technology. One of the first questions that a designer will ask when confronted with a design task is: what is to be the function of the thing? This use of the word function reminds us of mathematics. In math the concept of functions has to do with *transformations*. A mathematical function brings about a transformation from one number into another. The mathematical function $f(x) = x^2 + 2x + 1$ turns the number 1 into the number 4, it turns the number 2 into the number 9, etcetera. It looks rather artificial to recognize such a transition in the case of the bough and cane fulfilling the function of a support. But it is not impossible. Both transform a stroller with a bent, perhaps aching back into a happy, straight up walking person. For those who still find this to be a bit contrived, let us now look at other examples of functions, where the aspect of a transition is more evident. A coffee machine fulfills the function of making coffee. Here there is a clear transition, namely from the raw materials that are put into the machine into cups of tasty, warm coffee. This example can be multiplied by many others.

In general one can state that a technical function causes a change of one *situation or state* in to another. The first state is the one in which we find ourselves when we feel the need to use the artifact. Somehow we are not completely happy with this state and we are looking for a better one. We expect that we can reach this better state by using the artifact. We find ourselves at home, for example, but we would like to be in the grocery store because we want to buy some food. In that case we will use a transportation means, a car or a bike, to get from home to the grocery store. In other words, the car or bike fulfills the function of transforming our current state (being at home) into a desired one (being in the grocery store). The artifact enables us to perform an action that is necessary to realize the desired state.

Functions are closely related to human *intentions*. Because we have an intention to buy food, we want to realize the transformation that has been described above. The use of the word intention in philosophy is slightly different from our normal usage of language. We normally confine the meaning of the word intention to: being directed towards a certain purpose. But in philosophy the word has a wider meaning. It can be used for any form of being directed at something or someone. Intention is a state of the mind in which we are directed towards something or someone. This directness can have various characters. One we have met already: the directedness towards a purpose. Desiring something can also be called an intentional state of mind. We can be directed towards an object or state by desiring it. *Belief*, too, is called an intentional state of mind. Believing something about someone entails a sort of being directed toward that person, paying attention to him or her. Here we find ourselves in the field of the philosophy of mind.

In the case of an artifact there are at least two persons whose intentions are involved. In the first place there is the *designer*. She was the person that was responsible for the modification of what once was a natural object or material, although she may not have realized the modification herself (in our time, the designing and making of an artifact most of the times are done by different people). The designer had the intention of coming up with an artifact for fulfilling a practical purpose. In order to come up with a proper artifact the designer will have to consider the future intentions of the *user*: what is the practical purpose that he or she would like to see realized? A designer working in a household devices producing company may have the intention of designing a new device with which corks can be extracted from wine bottles. This designer then has to reflect on the wine lovers' intentions to open the bottle of wine. Once the product has been designed and manufactured the user will then take the device, in this case the corkscrew, and use it with the intention that the designer had anticipated. In order to stimulate proper use of the artifact, the designer may want to shape the artifact in such a way that it displays what it is meant for (here Dipert's idea about the difference between tools and artifacts are useful to consider).

Once the artifact is in the hands of the user, the designer has become powerless, apart from the influence that she can exert via the message that can be contained in the shape of the artifact or in the manual. It is now up to the user what to do with the artifact. In many cases he will use the artifact for the purpose that the designer had in mind when designing it. A screwdriver has been designed to turn screws and in many cases it will be used that way. But no one can stop the user from using it as a handy device with which tin can lids can be lifted. Admittedly, this is abhorrent for the well-educated professional, but down-to-earth hobbyists see no problem in doing that. The only comfort for the designer is that in the philosophy of technology we are willing to make a conceptual distinction between the two types of use that were mentioned. When the artifact is used in accordance with what the designer had in mind, we can say that it is used according to its *proper* function. When, however, the user employs the artifact in a different way, we can call that an *accidental* function. The other comfort for the designer may be that it is not unthinkable that the artifact will break down when not used according to its proper function. Screwdrivers may bend when used to open tin cans. But although the designer can be said to be right in the end, this, of course, does not make happy customers. Therefore designers will often not only think about the proper use of the device, but also try to anticipate accidental functions and design the device in such a way that it can stand all sorts of abuse ('abuse' in the designer's perception, of course). In other words, designers try to image what sort of *user plans* might come into existence once users have seen the artifact. Sometimes that is even a matter of great importance. In some countries producers of devices can be prosecuted when their products have harmed users, even in cases where the device was used improperly. In the USA, for example, a microwave oven producing company was sued by a lady who had put her dog into the microwave oven to dry it after it had had a bath. The designer had not anticipated this use and had failed to warn for it explicitly in the manual. Unbelievable as it may seem, the judge had put the lady in the right. It may drive designers crazy to think of the need to anticipate all the different ways of possible accidental use of their designs that may have dangerous effects. Users' intentions can be quite unforeseen, as the lady with her dog in the microwave oven proves. In this example, the use of the microwave was not only different from what the designer had intended, but also based on wrong ideas about the artifact.

It is also possible that after a certain time, the general use of an artifact shifts from what was intended to be the function by the designer (that is what we have called the proper function) to an accidental function. Such new use is not in accordance with what the designer intended (as in the microwave case), but it is not based on wrong ideas about the artifact (contrary to the microwave case), because the physical realization of the design does allow for that use, even though it was not the intended use. In that case one might question if it is still appropriate to call the function that the designer had in mind when designing the device still can be considered to be the 'proper' function in a situation where (almost) nobody still uses the artifact that way. In that case the meaning of the term 'proper' function should perhaps change into: what by a majority of users is considered to be 'proper'. In that case one would have to look for a different term to be used for the function that the designer had in mind. Philosopher John Searle has pointed out that there is indeed a certain *collective intentionality* involved in the ascription of functions to technical artifacts. We know the function of a hammer because there is a sort of collective belief that this device with its heavy short piece and its longer lighter end should be regarded to be a hammer. Searle has also pointed out that this collective intentionality is even more important when the functioning of the artifact has no relationship with the physical nature of it. A hammer is not only recognized as a hammer because of a collective intentionality but also because we can all individually guess from its physical nature that it is supposed to be a device for hammering nails into pieces of wood. But this is different in the case of e.g. a banknote. The functioning of the banknote has nothing to do with its physical nature (it could just as well have been a stone or a bar of gold). In that case the function of the artifact is entirely a matter of a collective belief that this piece of paper represents a certain value. The artifact has a symbolic meaning that is a result of this collective intentionality.

One of the sources of belief designers and user can have about a technical artifact is *perception* of the artifact. What do we perceive then? Well, we can see its shape, we can feel its surface characteristics (rough of smooth), we can perhaps smell it, we can exert force on it to see if it is strong, stiff and likewise we can test all sorts of mechanical properties. In general what we explore then are physical aspects of the artifact (and we will take that to include the chemical and biological aspects, if appropriate). We then try to set up a reasoning that takes us from the physical aspects to the functions that may be executed with the artifact. Suppose for the first time in our life we see a hammer lying on a table, we observe that it has a long part of a fairly light material (mostly wood) and a smaller, but much heavier part. From those physical characteristics we can guess that the long part is where we can take the artifact in our hand, and that the heavy part is suitable for exerting a strong force on something. When designing, the designer must have done the opposite. She has started with a desired function for the not yet existing artifact and has set up a line of reasoning to get from the function to optional physical aspects through which the desired function can be realized. Again in the example of the hammer: the designer realizes that the device needs to have a part that can be used to hold the hammer and a part with which we hit the nail. Then she reasons that the hammer needs to have a long part that we can hold and a heavy part with which a large impulse can be produced. Once the design has been made the designer too will reason from physical properties to functions in order to investigate if there are possible side-effects that may need to be avoided or perhaps enhanced. She may, for example, realize that the large impulse of the heavy part may cause it to get loose from the long part, which would cause a dangerous situation. Consequently, there has to be a strong connection between the long and the heavy part of the device.

We can formulate the considerations above in somewhat more general terms by stating that technical artifacts appear to have a *dual nature*. In the first place they are objects with physical properties, such as size, shape, color, weight, smell, chemical composition, etcetera. On the other hand they are objects that I can use for a certain function. This means that technical artifacts can be said to have both a *physical* and a *functional* nature. When designing and using the artifact we try to see connections between both natures. The designer seeks a physical nature (for a not yet existing artifact) that is fit for a desired functional nature, and when using the artifact the user identifies if the physical nature (of the existing artifact) is fit for a desired functional nature.

The relationship between physical and functional nature is never one to one predefined. For any desired functional nature, there are several options of physical natures, and vice versa. That is why creativity can play a role both in designing and using the artifact. This was not always recognized. In the Bauhaus approach, the *form follows function* rule was seen as determining the relationship between physical and functional nature. Once the function of an artifact to be designed has been determined, the form could be logically derived from that, according to this philosophy. Once it had been determined that a certain device should roll, it could be logically derived from this function that its shape should be round. But in the end it appeared to be impossible to apply this rule in all situations. Nowadays designers realize that for each function various forms can be created to fulfill that function. And vice versa: a certain form can be used for a variety of functions.

The fact that not all beliefs users have of artifacts (either of their physical or their functional nature) are true sometimes can be explained by the fact that the physical nature of the artifact is confusing to users. Research has shown that this is the case, for example, when *hybrid* products are involved. Hybrid products are devices that combine different functions. A well-known example is a Swiss pocketknife in which all sorts of functions can be present (knife, but also corkscrew, nail file, scissors, and small screwdriver). Another example is an alarm clock that has a radio too. It has been shown that the acceptance of such products by users depends on the extent to which the individual functions can be recognized. If users have difficulties in recognizing these functions from the physical appearance of the artifact, they will rather not buy the product. An example of such a failed product is a combination of a walkman and a field glass that had been designed by Sony. The phenomenon of such failing hybrid products again illustrates the need for designers to consider the intentions and beliefs of the future users.

Research into users' perceptions of artifacts is not only done by philosophers, but also by cognitive scientists. These scientists do empirical research into how people perceive products. Designers can use this information to anticipate possible wrong use of the artifact and to stimulate correct use. This will contribute to the customer satisfaction, because it prevents annoyance with the customer when the product does not function well due to wrong or inadequate use. Donald Norman, for example, shows how the design of door handles can either confuse users (when they try to open a door by pulling while actually it needs pushing) or help users (when the door handle is clearly shaped in such a way that it suggests pulling when pulling is needed, or pushing when pushing is needed). He also criticizes various designs in which the shape contains misleading suggestions about the possible use of the artifact. To illustrate this he uses the example of the four burners on the stovetop that are arranged in a square, while the four controls to operate them are organized in a linear way. This there is no relationship between the position of the burner and its accompanying control. This often leads to a wrong control to be switched on whereby even dangerous situations can emerge when a different burner starts burning than the one that was expected to burn. Norman has numerous other everyday examples to illustrate his point that designers often do not take into account the effects of the artifact's shape (or in general: its physical nature) on the perception the user develops about its functional nature.

More and more there is awareness in both the group of philosophers and of the cognitive scientists, of the possibility that their different disciplinary approaches to this issue could mutually benefit. Hence there is an increasing interaction between the philosophy of mind – that is the subdomain of philosophy that particularly deals with what minds are and how they function - and the cognitive sciences. Philosophy has a more theoretical, reflective approach, and cognitive sciences have an empirical approach, and these two can be complementary.

We also meet the concept of functions in the field of biology. When describing limbs organs biologists use the concept of functions. The heart is then said to have the function of pumping around the blood through the veins. In that case an analogy is drawn between the heart and a pump in, for instance, a central heating system. In the philosophy of biology there are many discussions about what is a proper description of functions in biology. These discussions have resulted in a number of options for that. Firstly there are those who say that the whole concept of functions does not belong to biology because it is related to intentions, and as they believe there should be no talking about intentions in biology. A second group of philosophers uses *etiological* accounts of functions. In this group we find philosophers like Ruth Millikan and Larry Wright. These are accounts in which a function is ascribed based on the role of a limb or organ in the evolutionary process. The function is what caused a particular shape of a limb or an organ to survive. These accounts look backwards. It is sometimes claimed that this natural process of selection is similar to the way a technical artifact emerges in the course of a historical process of try-outs and selection of the best option. A third group of philosophers, among whom Robert Cummins, uses forward-looking accounts of functions. In such accounts the function is the expectation of what the limb or organ will do in the organism or, more generally, in the whole system. This account seems to come closest to the way functions of technical artifacts are accounted for.

How does the use of the term function in biology then relate to the one in technology? Do we have a designer and user intention involved here too? Can we distinguish the difference between proper and accidental functions here too? The answer to those questions to a certain extent depends on the position one takes with respect to the 'design' of those limbs and organs. Roughly speaking, there are three possible positions. The first one is the acknowledgement of a real Designer, who had intentions and has created these limbs and organs accordingly. Among these are Christians or people of other religions who confess God as the Creator of all things, including those limbs and organs. Among them are scientists who use the complexity of the universe and its creatures that, according to their reasoning, cannot be adequately accounted for by mere chance. Intelligent Design is a name under which many of those scientists, among them William Dembski and Michael Behe have gathered. A second point of view is to acknowledge a designer, but to see the process of evolution to be that designer. Daniel Dennett is one of the better-known philosophers to take this stand. For him the heart and the mechanical pump are quite comparable, because in both cases a selection has been made for a design that best fulfills the function of pumping. As we humans ourselves in his view are just as well the outcome of a process of evolution, he sees no reason to make a difference between intentionality involved in the heart and in the mechanical pump. A third position is taken by those who claim that there is a difference in that the heart is not the result of intentional design and the mechanical pump is. These people usually agree with Dennett in seeing evolution in the process through which humans were created, but they do not want to give up the idea that humans, unlike evolution as a 'blind watchmaker' do have intentions of their own. Another question if whether one wants to ascribe intentions to the 'users' of the limbs and organs. To what extent can be said that a bird uses his wings intentionally? Here too, the answer largely is a matter of a choice that one cannot totally argue for. Some will say that men are different from animals in that they can have intentions and animals cannot. Others will claim that at least there are animals that can have intentions, and probably will point to chimpanzees that have been observed, for instance, to use sticks to reach for fruit. Again others will object that this need not be a proof of intention because it is comparable to certain types of birds that use stones to crack shells and that this is just a matter of following instincts rather than of conscious, intentional behavior.

It is clear that the number of functions that technical artifacts can have is endless. Therefore efforts have been made to bring some order into the chaos of all these different possible function by defining a limited number of function categories. An example of such a taxonomy is the following. Basic functions are: transporting, transforming, storing, retrieving, creating and destroying, connecting and separating. The claim that goes with such a taxonomy is that the function of each technical artifact can be analyzed in terms of combinations of these basic functions. A coffee bean grinder will then be a device in which we find the following basic functions: storing of the beans, transforming the beans into grains, storing the grains, retrieving the grains, transporting electrical energy from the net into the device, transforming electrical energy into mechanical energy, transforming information (the pushing of the 'on' button is transformed into an electrical connection that makes the electrical motor start). One could make a diagrammatic representation of the device by representing each function category by its own symbol. At first sight this seems to be a fairly unambiguous way of describing the device, but its practical use can be doubted. Designers so far have not been very interested in using such a representation.

Another way of differentiating between different kinds of functions can be found in the philosophical work of Herman Dooyeweerd, a Dutch philosopher. He came up with the concept of *qualifying function*. That is the function that tells us what the artifact is primarily meant for. The qualifying function of a banknote is an economic one: the banknote is primarily meant to be an artifact with an economic function. To show the variation of possible qualifying functions, he defined a set of fifteen aspects of reality, to which the qualifying function can refer. Some examples of those aspects are: the symbolical of linguistic, the economic, the juridical, the social, the pistic (that refers to beliefs, not necessarily religions). Let us take the example of a coin. For most coins the qualifying function is related to the economic aspect. But the coin that is fixed to a mayor's chain of office has a juridical qualifying function. And the shekels that were used in ancient times to pay the temple duties in Jerusalem had a pistic qualifying function (they could not be used for buying or selling outside the temple). Fake coins that are used in party games have a social qualifying function. For the designer it is important to know what the qualifying function of the artifact is to be. It makes a difference if a coin is to be used purely for a party game or if it is to be used as an official currency.

The full list of aspects is the following:

1. The arithmetical aspect
2. The spatial aspect
3. The kinematical aspect
4. The physical aspect
5. The biotic aspect
6. The sensitive aspect
7. The logical aspect
8. The historical aspect
9. The lingual aspect
10. The social aspect
11. The economic aspect
12. The aesthetic aspect
13. The juridical aspect
14. The ethical aspect
15. The pistic aspect

Another Dooyeweerdian concept can be used to describe the physical nature aspect of technical artifacts, namely the *subject and object functions*. Each artifact can serve as an object in all aspects. If it is sold, it serves as an object in the economic aspect. If it is appreciated for its beauty, it serves as an object in the aesthetical aspect. It can also serve as a subject, but not in all aspects. It can serve as a subject in the physical aspect, because it can act physically by itself. But it can not act as a subject in the economic aspect because it can not buy or sell by itself; it can only be bought or sold. For a mechanical device the physical aspect is the highest in which it can serve as a subject, for a biotechnological device this is the biotic aspect of the artifact. The difference can be significant: if the highest subject function is the physical aspect, the device needs maintenance; if it is the biotic aspect, it needs care, and that is not the same as maintenance, as any farmer with his heart at the right place can tell.

To illustrate how Dooyeweerd's concepts can result in an understanding of the nature of an artifact, Table 1 presents an analysis of various parts of a computer (microphone, display, IC or biochip, electromotor that rotates the harddisc) compared to some other objects (stones, sculptures, screwdrivers and chairs).

Table 2-1. Analysis of various objects in terms of their different types of functions

Object	Qualifying function	Highest subject function
Stone (in nature)*	Physical	Physical
Stone with crystal, used as a decoration at home**	Aesthetic	Physical
Sculpture***	Aesthetic	Physical
Screwdriver***	Historical	Physical
Chair***	Social	Physical
Banknote***	Economic	Physical
Microphone	Sensitive	Physical
Display	Lingual	Physical
Silicon IC	Logical	Physical
Biochip	Logical	Biotic
Electromotor	Kinematical	Physical
Wild plant	Biotic	Biotic
Greenhouse plant	Aesthetic	Biotic
Bio-engineered plant	Aesthetic	Biotic
Artificial plant	Aesthetic	Physical

* This is what Dipert calls a natural object.
** This is what Dipert calls an instrument
*** This is what Dipert calls a tool, and if it also displays information about its function, an artifact.

One more issue with respect to artifacts and functions is the question how technical artifacts can be distinguished from artifacts in art. It would be too easy to say that artifacts in art do not have practical purposes or functions. Serving as a decoration can be called a practical purpose or function no less than functions in technical artifacts. According to Dipert, one could have difficulties saying that a Rembrandt painting or a Michelangelo sculpture is 'used'. But he does not want to draw the conclusion that art artifacts have no function. For him artifacts in art only have a communicative-expressive function. But in practice it is not always easy to make the distinction.

3. TECHNICAL ARTIFACTS AS SYSTEMS

Most artifacts consist of more than one part. The idea that these artifacts have to work together to make the artifact as a whole fulfill its function, has led people to come up with the concept of *systems*. A system, roughly defined, is a *set* of parts that *work together*. A pair of scissors is a set of two parts working together. An airplane is a set of uncountable parts working together. Both can be called a system. But clearly they are quite different. For designing an airplane the concept of systems makes more sense to the designers, because of its complexity. Those designers will feel the need not only to work on the level of the system as a whole and the level of the individual parts, but to define intermediate levels of sub-systems (e.g. the power system of the plane) and sub-sub-systems (the power system for the cabin illumination), etcetera. The way the parts of the system are connected in fact is the 'physical nature' aspect of the system.

Apart from the way the parts of a system work together, there is a second way to conceptualize technological systems, namely by their *input, process* and *output*. This way of conceptualizing the system in fact is the 'functional nature' aspect of the system, because it shows the changes in state that the system brings about (and that was what functions were about). In German literature about systems, input and output are usually described in three components: *matter, energy* and *information*. A washing machine can thus be described as an artifact that takes in dirty laundry, clean water, detergent (these are materials), electrical energy and instructions for how to wash, given by the choice of washing program (information). The output of the machine is: clean laundry, dirty water with dissolved detergent (materials), heat and motion (energy), and a signal that indicates when the program has terminated (information). The process is a combination of heating the water, mixing the water and the detergent, rotating the drum, and so on. A designer will usually first consider the desired output (e.g. how clean should the laundry become), what is a convenient way of giving the input (e.g. how to put in the laundry and the detergent), and then to come up with a process (to be realized through a certain physical nature of the system) that transforms the convenient input into the desired output (in other words: that fulfills the desired function).

The systems approach to technical artifacts has been a dominant one for a certain period in the philosophy of technology. The concept of systems was seen as a most suitable one in the context of cybernetics: the science of controlling. In Chapter 5 we will refer again to this systems approach when dealing with the role of technology in society. For now it suffices to remark that the concept of *feedback* was important as an element in the systems concept. Engineers distinguish between positive and negative feedback. Positive feedback means that a change in output is reinforced by the feedback. A simple, non-technical example is the following. When I feel pain in my stomach, this makes me worry, which in turn will increase my pain. Positive feedback can lead to disasters. In a nuclear fission reactor an increase in temperature will cause an increase in the reaction rate and this will cause further increasing of the temperature, etcetera. This may lead to an explosion of the reactor. Negative feedback means that a change in the output is compensated. An example is the thermostat. When temperature increases and reaches a certain level, the heating will be switched off and the temperature will decrease until a certain level is reached and then the heating will be switched on again, etcetera. Negative feedback will lead to a sort of dynamic equilibrium.

4.   TEACHING AND LEARNING ABOUT TECHNICAL ARTIFACTS

For each of the chapters 2 through 6 we will end with some initial remarks about consequences of our philosophical reflections for teaching. These will really be some first and superficial ideas and in chapters 8 and 9 we will deal with these consequences more systematically. This final section in each of the chapters 2 through 6 is just to remind ourselves constantly that the background of our philosophical reflections is to support our teaching about technology.

In this chapter we have dealt with technology as artifacts. Artifacts can play an important role in teaching and learning about technology. In chapter 7 that will be described in more detail. Pupils and students can be stimulated to explore artifacts by taking them apart, watch their composition, the materials of which its components are made, and its possible functions. A deeper understanding of the artifact can be gained by realizing that the artifact has been designed in such a way that its physical nature fits its functional nature. An example of this is the teaching and learning about ancient devices and tools. By studying carefully their shape and materials, pupils and students can make estimations about the possible use of the ancient artifact. This is not always easy. It is known that the famous Smithsonian museum in Washington DC has a collection of artifacts, of which the function still is unknown to us. It is even unknown if the function was perhaps primarily symbolic. But for many artifacts it is possible to make sophisticated guesses about their functions.

The concept of systems can be a strong educational 'tool' to teach about artifacts, even in cases where engineers would perhaps not use it, at least not explicitly, when designing such an artifact. By making system diagrams of an artifact, its parts (sub-systems) and the way they are connected, pupils and students can get a first impression of the physical and the functional nature of the artifact. This, of course, requires a level of abstraction that makes this approach not suitable for all levels of education.

Chapter 3

TECHNOLOGICAL KNOWLEDGE

Artifacts, as we discussed them in the previous chapter, are the outcome of a process in which knowledge plays an important part. The nature of this knowledge has been a topic of controversy for many years already. Some philosophers have stated that the knowledge that is used by engineers to a large extent has been derived from science. This opinion usually is brought forward under the phrase "technology as applied science". Others, though, claim that technology has a body of knowledge of its own right and of a different nature than science. Their voice got stronger as criticism on the "technology as applied science" idea increased. Nowadays most philosophers will agree that at least part of what engineers know is of a different nature from what scientists know. But what then are the differences? In this chapter we will try to get an impression of that. Because most literature focuses on the knowledge of engineers I will also use the term 'engineering' most of the times in this chapters. But as stated in Chapter 1, this term is used only to separate out those professionals that create technology from all people that are involved in the process of adapting the natural environment according to human needs. Users also can be said to have technological knowledge, but less different types of knowledge. In order to get a view of the whole variety of types of technological knowledge, I have described the knowledge of engineers and I will assume that the knowledge that users have is a subgroup of the knowledge of engineers.

1.   WHAT IS KNOWLEDGE?

As we saw in chapter 1, epistemology is the sub-domain of philosophy that is concerned with knowledge. In this field most debates circle around the following short description of knowledge: *justified true belief.* The debates are about to extent to which this short description fits or does not fit with what we would like knowledge to be. Let us first consider what it means.

The short description mentioned above can be written somewhat more formal. We say that a person knows that p when:

1. the person believes that p;
2. the person has found justification for p;
3. p is true.

The letter 'p' stands for *proposition.* A proposition is the content of a statement about something. "Today it rains" is a proposition, but also "Tomorrow it will rain". As a proposition is the content of a statement, the proposition 'it rains' in English is considered to be the same as the proposition 'il pluit' in French or the proposition 'es regnet' in German. Engineers use lots of propositions, like "The stiffness of cast iron is . . .", or "In order to be resistant against rain, a car body needs to be coated". When do we say, that an engineer 'knows' these things? In the first place that engineer must believe that these things are so. If (s)he does not even believe it, how can you say (s)he knows it? Furthermore, the engineer must have sought some sort of justification for believing it. That can be in that (s)he read about it in a professional journal, or (s)he has learnt in it her professional training, or perhaps by experience. The final condition is that the statement must be true. When I make the statement that it is now three o'clock because I sincerely believe that and I have found evidence for it by watching a clock, we still refuse to call that 'knowledge' in case the clock does not function and it is now four o'clock. But what if I have read the clock coincidentally when it was indeed three o'clock? Then all conditions 1 through 3 are fulfilled, but still we do not want to call this 'knowledge'. This example shows that the original definition of knowledge is not sufficiently accurate. In the course of time, various philosophers have tried to 'repair' the definition by adding more conditions, but so far there is no generally accepted definition, and some philosophers even claim that the whole idea of justified true belief needs to be abandoned.

Alvin Plantinga, who uses a terminology that seems to have come straight from technology, offers one interesting alternative. According to him, knowledge means the following:

1. a person believes that p (as in the 'traditional' definition of knowledge),
2. the person's belief is the result of proper functioning cognitive faculties (that is: they function according to their design plan),
3. the person's cognitive faculties function in an environment that is suitable for their proper functioning,
4. the person's cognitive functioning were aimed at truth (not at e.g. believing what one would like to believe),
5. the design plan for the cognitive faculties was a good plan,
6. p is true (note that this is the same as the third condition in the 'traditional' definition of knowledge).

Conditions 2-5 are what Plantinga indicates as *warrant*. Plantinga's main motive for developing this complex definition is that he believed that sound foundations for knowledge can never be found only in the knowing person, but must be sought outside him or her. It is not enough to seek this foundation in the knowing person's beliefs and in his or her fulfilling an obligation to find justification. Knowledge must be established 'from outside', by watching if the person's capacities to know function well and according to their purpose. Plantinga opts for what one can call an *externalist* rather than an *internalist* approach. It is interesting to note that Plantinga uses at least two terms that play an important part technology: proper function and design plan. We have already discussed the first in Chapter 2. The second will be dealt with in Chapter 4.

2.   TECHNOLOGICAL KNOWLEDGE

Whatever extra condition one would add to the justified true belief account of knowledge, technological knowledge does not fit well with this definition. There are several reasons for that. In the first place, there is technological knowledge that cannot be expressed properly in propositions. When a carpenter says that he knows how to hit the nail at exactly the right spot in order to make it go strait into the wood, he probably cannot tell that in words. He will rather say something like: "well, I just know that; I do not know exactly how, but I just feel how to do it". Gilbert Ryle, based on this sort of considerations, has defined a distinction between *knowing-that* and *knowing-how*. Knowing-that is the knowledge that we can express in propositions, and for which the 'justified true belief' account could fit, and knowing-how is knowledge that cannot be expressed in propositions. Skills clearly are of the knowing-how type.

Another part of technological knowledge that cannot be expressed in propositions is the knowledge that engineers express in their sketches and drawings. This is what Ferguson called 'the mind's eye': knowledge that needs to be *visualized*. Sketches and drawings contain a richness of knowledge that could never be entirely expressed in propositions. This representation of knowledge is one where the difference between novices and experts can be recognized. Research has indicated that experts tend to see larger patterns of information, whereas novices tend to focus on details. This has to do with the fact that experts have learnt to organize their knowledge in networks of concepts, whereas for novices the integration of a newly learnt concept into a larger network of already existing knowledge yet has to take place. This difference also holds for the propositional types of knowledge.

Apart from the reasons that have been mentioned above, another reason for questioning the validity of the 'justified true belief' account of knowledge for technological knowledge is that engineers also have knowledge about norms. *Normativity* is also characteristic for knowledge of functions. When an engineer says: "I know that this is a device that can be used for hammering a nail into the wood" (which is mostly expressed more briefly as: "I know that this is a hammer") in this statement a normative judgment is included: the engineer claims that the device is good for hammering a nail into the wood. But how can norms be said to be 'true'? Norms can be effective and efficient, but not true or false, at least not in a realist account of knowledge. Here we touch on a very fundamental issue in epistemology and ontology. In a *realist* account it is taken for granted that there is a reality outside us that can be perceived and about which we can have knowledge. In this view we can know something because it exists. The alternative vision is based on the assumption that something exists only because we have beliefs about it. This is the *anti-realist* account. In this account theories do not refer to a reality behind what we have observed, but only to our observations. Truth in the realist account means that our knowledge is a correct image of (in other words: corresponds to) reality. In an anti-realist or instrumental vision it is no more than an effective way of accounting for what we have observed. In the case of the realistic vision norms do not refer to an existing reality but to one that is not (yet) there. In that case there is no correspondence between the knowledge and existing reality. Because their involvement with reality involves more than observation (as in the case of a scientist) but also manipulation, probably most engineers – either consciously or not – will take a realist stance. It should be noted here that the description of the realist versus anti-realist discussion is a lot more complex, but for the sake of an general introduction it suffices to recognize that there are different opinions about the relationship between our knowledge and reality, and that engineers will probably tend to believe in the existence of a reality that is independent of their perception and knowledge (at least, as far as descriptive knowledge is concerned; when it comes to prescriptive knowledge, engineers often take a more instrumental stance, as we will se further on).

Norms in technological knowledge can apply at various levels. We can say: "I know that this particular hammer is a good for getting a nail into a piece of wood". In that case the norm is applied to one single case (a *token*) of all possible hammers. We can also say: "I know that all hammers of this brand are good for getting a nail into a piece of wood". I that case the norm is applied to a *type* of hammers rather than one token of a type. Finally we can say that all hammers are good for getting a nail into a piece of wood. In that case the norm is applied in the widest sense. It is clear that these propositions really express different kinds of technological knowledge. It requires much more experience (either gained by myself or by others who inform me about their experiences) to be able to say that all hammers of a certain brand are good for getting a nail into a piece of wood than to say only that this particular hammer is good for that.

Finally, it can be questioned if 'truth' is the primary condition that engineers are interested in when they seek for knowledge. Perhaps adequacy, efficiency, effectiveness are much more appropriate conditions for engineers to use when looking for knowledge. For example: when a civil engineer designs a new bridge, she knows that quantum mechanics is a true theory about the materials and forces in the bridge. But it would be useless to try to use that. Rather she would use classical mechanics, which strictly spoken is not true, but is sure is much more efficient to be used in the design process. And in the past designing bridges was even a matter of blindly following rules of thumb about the internal dimensioning of the bridge. That sort of knowledge can hardly be assessed in terms of true or false, as has been remarked before already.

One alternative for the belief account of technological knowledge, of which we have seen that it only partially fits with the nature of technological knowledge, is to characterize certain examples of technological knowledge as acceptances rather than as beliefs. Acceptances are claimed to be important in particular for practical reasoning (more than in theoretical reasoning). And as technology to a large extent is a matter of practical reasoning, the concept of acceptances is certainly worth examining for it fitness to describe the nature of technological knowledge. Philosophers like Michael Bratman and Pascal Engel have formulated differences between beliefs and acceptances as follows:

- beliefs are involuntary, acceptances are voluntary. Once you have perceived a crack in the surface of a device, you must believe there is a crack in that surface. But accepting or rejecting a rule that says when the crack needs to be repaired in order to prevent possible accidents is a matter of your own decision;
- beliefs aim at truth, acceptances aim at utility. When I believe that copper conducts electricity, I do so because I think it is worth believing that because it is true. But when I accept the rule that copper wire can be used in electrical devices I do so because I think that rule is worth accepting because of its practical use;
- beliefs are shaped by evidence, acceptances are shaped by other considerations such as prudence. I believe that a certain material can burn, because I have done experiments that created evidence for this belief. But I accept certain rules for not using such materials in places where fire can emerge and create a dangerous situation and I do so because of prudence.
- beliefs are context-independent, whereas acceptances are context-dependent. My belief that the material can burn remains the same when I travel abroad or when years have passed (unless of course there has emerged evidence against it). But whether I accept the rule not to use such material when designing an artifact depends on the situation. Sometimes I will accept that rule because the specific situations requires it, but in other occasions I may decide that the rule makes no sense there and therefore I will reject it for that situation;
- beliefs must together form a coherent whole, whereas acceptances need not fulfill that requirement. If I believe a certain material is a semiconductor, it must be possible to integrate that belief with other beliefs about the same material that together give me a coherent picture of what the material is like. But I can accept all sorts of rules about that material that need not be integrated in order to yield a new total rule about how to deal with the material. Of course the rules I accept must not be inconsistent with each other, but no need is felt to integrate them into an overall rule.
- beliefs come in degrees, acceptances are an 'all-of-nothing' matter. My belief that wood is a suitable material for making furniture grows the more experiences I gain in designing and making wooden furniture. But

accepting the rule that a wooden chair must always be polished before delivery is something I do or I do not do it.

Technological knowledge of rules (prescriptive knowledge) often seems to be more acceptance-like than belief-like, particularly because a lot of technological knowledge has to do with rules (here again we see the normative element in much technological knowledge).

We have now seen that technological knowledge has certain characteristics that make it different from scientific knowledge. To get an idea of the content of technological knowledge, we will explore different taxonomies for technological knowledge. The first one has been developed by Walther Vincenti is his book "What Engineers Know and How The Know It". This book contains a collection of historical case studies in aeronautics, in particular in aircraft design. From those case studies Vincenti derived six categories of technological knowledge:

1. *fundamental design concepts* (operational principles and normal configurations),
2. *design criteria and specifications,*
3. *theoretical tools* (mathematics, reasoning, laws of nature),
4. *quantitative data* (descriptive and prescriptive),
5. *practical considerations* and
6. *design instrumentalities* (procedural knowledge).

If we take the design of a car as an example, we can recognize all of these categories. Fundamental design concepts mean that a car designer immediately has a basic image of a car in his or her mind: an object with four wheels, a body, an engine, and so on. The designer also has knowledge about what conditions the car should fulfill: e.g. what speed, what safety regulation. Theoretical tools in this example are laws of mechanics, but also the CAD program that is used to design the car. Knowledge of quantitative data entails knowledge of material properties. Practical considerations are based on the designers' experience and may be such considerations as to choose a certain color for the car based on a good feeling for what would fit with people's aesthetical preferences. Knowledge of design instrumentalities (or procedural knowledge) here is the knowledge of the sequence of actions that is needed in the design process of a car. Although the taxonomy is based on a limited set of cases, it seems that the categories cover pretty well the variety of issues that an engineer may have knowledge of.

Vincenti went one step further and identified the origin of the various categories of technology: how do engineers get to know the content of the various categories? As possible sources of engineering knowledge he identified: transfer from science, invention, theoretical and experimental engineering research, design practice, production and direct trial. In his analysis he shows that the contribution of transfer from science is very limited. Most knowledge comes from other sources. And even when transferred from science, the knowledge often needs quite a transformation in order to become useable for the engineer. Abstract concepts in e.g. thermodynamics need to be translated into more concrete and practical concepts in order to be useable in the design of an aircraft. This analysis shows that technology can not be claimed to be just applied science. There is more involved in technology than just scientific theories. Science, though, can do more than deliver theories to technology. Science can have a *heuristic* role in technology. That means it can help to identify what variables may be relevant to study and manipulate in a design process. For example, we can learn from science what variables determine the pressure around objects, and from that we can learn what variables can be used to optimize the lift force of a wing of an aircraft. This is a weaker function for science than delivering ready-to-be-used theories about how these variables determine the lift force, but still it can be a very useful function in engineering design work.

A different way of gaining insight into the variety of things engineers can know, the dual nature of artifacts can be used. In Chapter 3 we have explored this idea and now we will use it to develop a more systematic and hopefully a more complete taxonomy of technological knowledge than Vincenti's case study based taxonomy. Roughly speaking, engineers can have knowledge of the physical nature of the artifact (e.g. knowledge of its material properties), knowledge of its functional nature (knowledge of what is means to function as a hammer or a screwdriver), and knowledge of the relationship between the physical nature and the functional nature (e.g. knowing that a certain material property makes a device suitable for using it for a certain purpose). A fourth type of knowledge can be the knowledge of processes that are involved in the functioning or in the making of the artifact (e.g. knowledge of the sequence of steps in which a corkscrew can extract a cork from a wine bottle neck).

This is a very concise taxonomy, and perhaps a bit too concise for practical use. We can extend it by applying Dooyeweerd's aspects of reality, which we have met in Chapter 2. Then we get the following taxonomy:

a) Knowledge of the physical nature (non-intentional aspects, in which the artifact can serve as a subject)
   i) The arithmetical aspects
   ii) The spatial aspects
   iii) The kinematical aspects
   iv) The physical aspects
   v) The biotic aspects
b) Knowledge of the functional nature (intentional aspects, in which the artifact can only serve as an object to which a subject ascribes a function)
   i) The sensitive aspects
   ii) The logical aspects
   iii) The historical aspects
   iv) The lingual aspects
   v) The social aspects
   vi) The economic aspects
   vii) The aesthetic aspects
   viii) The juridical aspects
   ix) The ethical aspects
   x) The pistic aspects

This extended taxonomy offers a more detailed picture of the complexity of the knowledge that is needed to design the artifact than the division into only the physical and the functional aspects yields. A designer ideally would take into account all these aspects. Of course that is not always possible, and fortunately there are cases in which only a limited subset of all categories is of importance, and the others have less impact. If we take for example the design of a computer, we can recognize the various aspects that the engineer can have knowledge of: the computer works with only 0's and 1's (arithmetical aspect), it takes a certain space of the desk or on your lap (spatial aspect), it must have moving parts (kinematical aspect), it has properties such as weight, hardness, strength (physical aspect), it is not a living thing itself, but it has to interact with living things (biotic aspect), it will be watched and touched (sensitive aspect), it is based on rules that humans have developed (logical aspect), it has been developed over a period of years (historical aspect), we interact with it by using languages (lingual aspect), it can connect people (social aspect), it has a price tag (economic aspect), it has a certain appearance that people may like or dislike (aesthetic aspect), it's design is protected by patents (juridical aspect), there are issues of privacy in the access of data that it contains (ethical aspect) and it has given rise to strong beliefs in the power of technology (pistic aspect). Many of these aspects do need to be taken into account when designing the computer.

When designing an artifact the designer uses these various types of knowledge. It is thanks to this knowledge that artifacts become what they become. One could almost say that the knowledge has been 'absorbed' by the artifact. And someone using the artifact by examining it closely can sometimes recognize what knowledge probably has been used to determine the shape and the materials of the artifact. But for someone not having the expertise to recognize what knowledge is in the artifact, the knowledge has just 'disappeared'. The knowledge is now as it were embodied in the artifact. This made Davis Baird, a philosopher of technology, create a special term for this phenomenon: thing knowledge. Thing knowledge is fairly specific for technology. In science the knowledge usually refers to phenomena and not to artifacts (although phenomena of course are observed in and through artifacts).

3.   ENGINEERING SCIENCES

So far we have seen that technology is different from science when we consider the aspect of knowledge. The difference is understandable when we realize that science and technology have different purposes: science aims at developing new knowledge about reality as it is, while technology aims at changing reality according to our needs and desires. This difference also has consequences for the knowledge in these two domains. Apart from the differences that we have already seen, we can say that science works with *abstraction* and *idealization* in order to make reality more fit for mathematical description. When a physicist describes a falling object in the simple formula for linearly accelerated motions, she will abstract from all sorts of non-physical aspects (for example, to her it will make no difference whether the falling object is a dead stone or a living cat) and she will work with a frictionless air (which is an idealization, of course). Technology on the other hand almost by definition has to work with the *concrete* reality and its full *complexity*. Another difference is that scientific knowledge is *universal*: it does not matter whether you are on earth, on the moon, in water or air: the formula for gravity is always the same (only the gravity constant differs between different situations). Technological knowledge usually is more *specific*: it is related to one specific situation and not automatically applicable to all other situations.

Yet in the course of time, a relationship between science and technology has grown, with consequences for both of them. Science has changed dramatically through the use of technological devices (e.g. measurement equipment). Technology has been influenced by scientific methodology. Nowadays engineers also make abstractions and idealizations to solve practical problems (although at some point, of course, the will always have to return to concrete and non-ideal situations). One could say that technology has become more scientific in its approach. Sometimes this is visible in the outcomes of the process. Mass production and standardization lead to products that are all the same, and thus has a universal character, similar to the universal nature of scientific knowledge. No matter if you are in Amsterdam, Paris, Washington DC or Hong Kong, a Big Mac looks the same and tastes the same.

The influence of science on technology has also led to new scientific disciplines, the *engineering sciences*. In those sciences, knowledge is developed that goes beyond the individual technological problem and can be used for a wider range of problems. This gives the engineering sciences a peculiar character compared to most other sciences. Some sciences are *nomo-thetical*, that is, they seek to state laws that hold for all places and all times. Natural sciences are a good example of such sciences. Other sciences are *ideo-graphical*, that is, they seek to describe the particularities rather than the generalities. History is a good example of such sciences, because history seeks to describe particular events rather than general laws or patterns in history. The engineering sciences seem to be somewhat in between. On the one hand they seek laws and rules that transcend individual design problems, but on the other hand they should not get too far removed from practical situations and a too high level of generality would hamper that. There is a second distinction between types of sciences that engineering sciences seem to violate. Some sciences seek to describe causal relationships, while other relationships seek to describe intentions of people and their effects. Natural sciences are a good example of the first types. Even when phenomena are studied that we can see with people as well as with dead matter, the intention of the people is not taken into account in natural sciences. For some time it was popular to take the same approach in psychology and treat people as 'things' that would produce a certain response to a certain stimulus. Now that approach has been abandoned in psychology (at least by the large majority of psychologists) and this science is now seen as a science in which intentions of people should be taken into account. Engineering sciences again seem to be difficult to be put under one of the two headings. On the one hand, cause-effect relations are studied often in engineering sciences, for instance when material properties are examined, but on the other hand, intentions of people, such as customer requirements, also play a vital part in engineering sciences, in particular when design activities are concerned. It is evident that engineering sciences are of a peculiar nature and really different from other types of sciences.

In spite of the fact that the engineering sciences may not fit well in the usual types of sciences (nomothetical or ideographical, concerned with cause-effect relations or with intentions), we do accept them as genuine sciences, and therefore we expect that knowledge will evolve in ways that are similar to the way knowledge evolves in other sciences. In the philosophy of science, the way scientific knowledge grows is examined. As the development of scientific knowledge in the engineering disciplines can be expected to show patterns similar to those that have been found in other disciplines, it makes sense to explore the insights that have been gained in the philosophy of science with respect to the development of scientific knowledge if we want to get to know how engineering sciences work.

There are a number of different approaches to develop scientific knowledge. These differences are related to what one accepts as scientific knowledge. In the first approach, the *positivist* approach, only what has been observed objectively is accepted as scientific knowledge. What goes beyond that, such as hypotheses about cause-effect relationships related to the observed phenomena, is metaphysical speculation. The use of mathematics and logic is allowed, but only to combine observed facts in more economical ways of presentation (for example to replace a long table of observations by a simple mathematical expression). This most certainly is an approach that we find in the engineering sciences. Engineers have at their disposal thick handbooks that contain lots of long tables with all sorts of observed and measured data. A construction engineer can look up data for various sorts of woods when constructing a wooden house. In such a case there is no need to look for cause-effect relationships. The mere table and its data are sufficient for the need of the engineer.

But more is needed than handbooks with tables. There are lots of situations in which ideas about causes and effects are crucial for solving engineering problems. In such cases the positivist approach will not work. Strictly speaking the positivist is not allowed to make claims for situations that have not been observed. In such cases engineers need a different approach. The *empirical-deductive* approach offers an alternative for such cases. In this approach hypotheses are developed, from the hypothesis it is derived (deduced) what the outcome of a certain empirical experiment should be in order to confirm the hypothesis and then the experiment is carried out to test the hypothesis. As long as no outcomes of experiments clash with the hypothesis, it can be maintained as a possible explanation of a phenomenon, and to predict what will happen in a certain situation for which the hypothesis can be used. In this way a lot of knowledge has been developed in engineering sciences, and is used to predict e.g. if a design will function according to the criteria and specifications. Popper, a famous 20th century philosopher of science, has claimed that in order for a hypothesis to be scientific it needs to be *falsifiable*. In other words, it should be possible to think up a possible experiment, of which one of the possible outcomes is that the hypothesis must be rejected. To illustrate this idea, Popper uses the example of swans in a forest. The hypothesis that in this forest there are only white swans is acceptable in terms of falsifiability, because I can imagine an experiment of which a possible outcome is that the hypothesis appears not to be true, namely going into the wood and inspecting each swan one sees for its color. Then it is possible that I will come across a black swan, which will lead me to do away with the hypothesis or replace it by a new one: all swans in this forest are either white or black. This hypothesis again is acceptable in terms of falsifiability and is clearly a step forward with respect to the previous one. Hypotheses that do not fulfill the condition of falsifiability for Popper have too much of dogma's that will never be given up, in spite of the facts. Those who read horoscopes will recognize this: most of the time they have been phrased in such a way that they will always become true somehow. Their predictive value then of course is almost zero, and this is another objection against non-falsifiable hypotheses. In engineering we often feel the need to test hypotheses. In fact each design or prototype can be seen as a sort of hypothesis: we expect that it will fulfill the desired function, and this 'theory' can be tested by trying out the design or prototype. If the design or prototype works, our 'hypothesis' can be maintained, and if it fails, we will have to come up with a new 'hypothesis', that is a new design or prototype. There is a difference, though, between using this approach is (natural) sciences and in engineering. In sciences the hypothesis always will have to undergo new tests because we can never be sure that we have overlooked a possible test that will falsify the hypothesis. In engineering, to the contrary, we are justified to finish testing as soon as the design has proved to function in the context for which it was designed. This reveals a difference is approach between science and engineering: scientists are *problem-oriented* (they want to keep exploring the problem) and engineers are *solution-oriented* (as soon as a good satisfying has been found, the problem is no longer of interest).

But in practice hypothesis are not always given up as soon as the first counterproof appears. To illustrate that Thomas Kuhn, another well-known philosopher of science (although many people rather call him a sociologist of science) uses the example of classical mechanics at the end of the 19th century. By then classical mechanics had shown to be a powerful theory with which many phenomena could be described well, and for that reason it was not easily given up when facts about very small and very fast moving particles were found that contradicted classical mechanics. But at a certain moment the amount of such facts was large enough to make the whole scientific community move from classical to relativistic mechanics and quantum mechanics. This is what Kuhn calls a revolution from one *paradigm* (classical mechanics) to another paradigm (relativistic and/or quantum mechanics). In between two revolutions there is a fairly stable period of what Kuhn calls *normal science*. According to Kuhn such transitions were mainly the result of sociological factors (e.g. who has most influence), but Imre Lakatos disagreed with that and claimed that there are good reasons to move from one paradigm to the other. He came up with the idea of theories being treated as research programs, in which a theory is assessed on the basis of its fruitfulness (either because it brings about new knowledge and theories, or because its applications are good). In engineering sciences this means that a theory can be assessed on the basis of its applications: if the design for which those theories were used, hold, the theory can be kept.

Do we find paradigms and revolutions in engineering sciences? Yes, indeed. That can be illustrated by examining the dominant theories about the design of buildings in architecture. Each style period can be seen as a period in which a certain style (for instance gothic, baroque, neoclassicism, postmodernism) is treated as a paradigm that is no easily given up. But at a certain moment in a relatively short time the 'world of architects' as a whole moves from one paradigm to the next. But in other areas we find paradigms too. Edward Constant has studied the development of the turbojet engine and concluded from his data that this too can be seen as a paradigm shift compared to existing types of engines. One could defend that in this respect technology develops in a way that is very similar to science: there can be a long period of *normal engineering* (analog to 'normal science') until in a relatively short time the whole engineering community decides to change toward a new (technological) paradigm in what can be called a revolution, after which again a period of 'normal engineering' begins, but now based on the new paradigm.

Finally there is a more loose approach that has been proposed by e.g. Paul Feyerabend. According to him 'anything goes' when it comes to the development of scientific knowledge. Feyerabend does not believe in 'the' scientific method, whatever it might be. He sees anarchy as the best way of reaching new scientific insights. That is something we can also recognize in engineering. Vincenti's sources of engineers' knowledge suggest pretty loose ways of gaining that knowledge. Accidental experiences in designing and making artifacts according to him even contribute to a wider range of engineering knowledge categories than transfer from science. Scientific research problems are often better articulated than technological problems. Many times scientists have a pretty clear view of what relationship between what variables is to be examined. Engineers are often faced with much more open-ended and undefined problems. No wonder that Feyerabend's approach appeals to engineers, even though they may never have heard of it.

One of the things engineering sciences has in common with other sciences is the use of modeling and analogies. In engineering sciences we find different types of models for different purposes. In general a model is a representation of a reality (of a real artifact or of a real phenomenon) that has certain characteristics of the real thing, but has been modified with respect to other characteristics. For example, a model of a tall building can have the same shape as the real building, but the size has been modified. In this case the purpose of the modeling is to enable the building to be tested empirically on e.g. wind patterns around the building. Rather than trying to measure winds around the real building, we make a scale model and put it in a wind tunnel. We then have to take into account that by changing the size of the building in the model, we may also have changed other properties, some of which may have an influence on the validity of the outcomes on the model for the real situation. In the case of a scale model, not only the size changes, but also the surface/volume ratio. For some experiments that may be of importance for a proper interpretation of the outcomes. Always when using models we have to realize that the model is only analogous to reality in certain respects. We can distinguish different types of analogies:

- *shape analogies*: the shape of the maquette is the same as the shape of the real city section that is yet to be built;
- *structural analogies*: the structure of an electron microscope is analogous to the structure of a light microscope (there is a similar set of lenses in a similar setting),
- *functional analogies*: the switch in an electrical circuit has the same function as the tap in a water circuit;
- *formal analogies*: the formula for the gravitational force between two masses is analogous to the electrical force between two electrical charges.

One has to be careful not to mix up these types of analogies. When the transistor was developed in the 1940s, the researchers had the idea of copying the structure of the tube triode (a cathode, an anode, and a grid in between) in solid state material. They expected that this shape analogy would be accompanied by a functional analogy (that the solid state cathode, anode and grid would function in the same way the cathode, anode and grid in the tube triode did). But this idea was falsified when they found out that their solid state version of the triode did not work as expected, and due to the lack of understanding of what happened in the material, they were not able to miniaturize the device. This example shows that the different types of analogies should be treated differently.

Analogies can be used to make different types of models:

- *physical models*: models made from materials to represent things (such as the miniature airplane that is tested in the wind tunnel),
- *graphical models*: drawings that are used to represent e,g, buildings or electrical circuits,
- *numerical models*: models that represent the quantitative aspects of things (e.g. a Finite Element Method, FEM, model that is used to calculate, among other things, stresses in materials).

Models can have different functions in engineering. Sometimes models are used to develop theories or designs. The simplification that the model offers helps to get grips on the design problem. We leave out a number of aspects in order to be better able to describe the others. Such models are always a *reduction* of the real world situation, because we have left out things. Other models are used for the aim of testing theories or designs. The model than offers the opportunity to do experiments that we can not do in the real world situation, for example because an artifact is too small or to large to be tested experimentally. The use of models particularly confronts us with the tension that we find in engineering sciences between idealizing and abstracting as a means for developing and testing theories and designs, and on the other hand the need to have concrete and exact knowledge because in the end it is the full complex reality that we have to manipulate in engineering.

4. TRANSFER AND INTEGRATION OF KNOWLEDGE IN TECHNOLOGY

One of the characteristics of technology is that it involved quite different knowledge domains. Design problems not only call for knowledge of technical data, but also for knowledge about what customers want, what legislation allows, what amount of money is available, and lots of other aspects. The Dooyeweerd-inspired analysis has even fifteen different aspects, each of which is studied in a separate scientific discipline. Mathematics deals with the arithmetic and the spatial aspects, physics with the kinematical and the physical aspects, biology with the biological aspects, and so on. If knowledge about all those aspects is to be involved in technological work, this means that a whole variety of scientific disciplines is to be involved. In our analysis of technological knowledge, we have assumed that engineers have knowledge of those aspects also, but of course to a limited extent, and by far not with the specialized expertise of scientists in those various non-technological disciplines. Therefore engineers have to 'borrow' (or, more formally stated, *transfer*) knowledge from other disciplines and *integrate* that with their own knowledge. Vincenti has already shown for transfer from scientific knowledge that this is a process in which the knowledge often needs a certain *transformation* in order to become usable for the engineer. We can expect that this it the same for knowledge transfers from other disciplines.

There are various levels of integrating knowledge from various disciplines. An example of a taxonomy for that has been presented by Margaret Boden. She identifies the following levels of *interdisciplinarity*:

1. Encyclopedic: in this type knowledge of various disciplines is available, but researchers do not necessarily make use of them (a university as a totality is mentioned as an example of this),
2. Contextualizing: people take some account of other disciplines in teaching and determination of research goals, but without active research co-operation,
3. Shared: people from different disciplines work together on a complex problem, but not as close as in day-to-day co-operation,
4. Co-operative: people from different disciplines actively work together towards a common goal,
5. Generalizing: people from different disciplines share common theoretical perspectives that are applied to their disciplines,
6. Integrated: concepts and insights of one discipline contribute to the work that is done in another discipline vice versa.

Clearly the way these levels are defined is very much on the basis of the extent to which humans as bearers of knowledge do or do not co-operate. In fact this is a *social epistemology* approach to the issue of knowledge integration. The popularity of that approach to a certain extent is due to the difficulties in defining what a *discipline* is in terms of its knowledge. Several efforts have been made to do that. One could try to define what physics is by adding a number of theories like mechanics, optics, thermodynamics, and electrodynamics and calling that collection 'physics'. But constantly there are new theories that do not fit so well in those sub-domains and make it problematic to say whether or not they belong to physics in that way of defining the discipline. Another strategy is to define a discipline in terms of its research methods. But that is equally problematic. Who would be able to identify exactly what makes physics different from biology in terms of its research methods? Yes, we treat them as different disciplines at university level (you can study either one, but not both at the same time). Because of these difficulties people nowadays tend to define what a discipline is in social terms: a discipline exists when there is a community of researchers that calls themselves after that discipline (e.g. 'economists'), have international journals and conferences, have faculties or departments named after them, and the like. Boden's way of identifying levels of interdisciplinarity clearly refers to that approach.

In technology this spectrum of integration levels can certainly be recognized. Sometimes technological developments take place as the work of a small, disciplinary team, while other, more complex developments, require large teams in which several disciplines work together intensely. It makes quite a difference if a new chemical is designed that has certain new properties, based on the molecular structure of the new chemical, or if a team of engineers designs a whole factory for mass-producing that chemical. In the first process mainly chemical engineering knowledge is needed, while in the second process aspects safety regulations, costs, environmental legislation, and numerous other technical and social aspects have to be taken into account, for which specialized knowledge of various disciplines is needed. The 'weaker' forms of interdisciplinarity, in which in fact each of the individual remains unaffected by the other disciplines, can also be called *multidisciplinarity*, because it entails a multiplicity of disciplines rather than the emergence of a new field of knowledge that is situated between the existing disciplines.

5.   TEACHING TECHNOLOGICAL KNOWLEDGE

The differences between scientific and technological knowledge no doubt have consequences for teaching technological knowledge. In this section we will explore what those consequences may be.

In the first place we have to realize that not all technological knowledge can be taught by presenting propositions to the learners (e.g. in textbooks or in oral instructions). Part of technological knowledge cannot, as we have seen, be expressed in propositions. Such knowledge must be taught and learnt in a different way. Probably learning-by-doing is the best way for that. It reminds of the relationship between apprentice and master in the medieval guilds. The master would teach skills to the apprentice by demonstrating and than watching the apprentice imitating him, and correcting the apprentice until he sufficiently mastered the skill. At least part of the process of teaching and learning technological knowledge must be done in that way. Textbooks are no option for teaching and learning knowledge that cannot be adequately expressed in propositions. Pictures can play a supportive role here. Pictures are not propositions and they may be a useful complement in the process of oral instruction and demonstrating the skills.

In the second place we have seen that normative aspects are intrinsic in technological knowledge. That characteristic of technological knowledge should be mirrored in teaching and learning about technology. It means that this teaching and learning always comprises the aspect of judging and assessing. Technological knowledge does not take things as they are, but give a normative opinion about them. Pupils and students should not only learn what a certain device is, but also what is should be like and what we would consider to be malfunctioning. Pupils and students should not only learn material properties (sec), but also what material properties make materials suitable for what purpose. And although at first sight most of the normativity in technological knowledge does not directly have an ethical character, ethics can be nearby when one investigates the origins of the norms that are used. What we call a 'good' car can be seen as a purely functional characterization. But someone who is active in an environmental pressure group will refuse to use that qualification if it is known that the car causes more environmental damage than other similar cars. And then we are a whole lot closer to ethics then we had originally estimated. Those who are involved in the teaching about technology should not abstain from implementing normative issues in their teaching. There are people who reject this and state that there should be no indoctrination in teaching. But teaching about normativity does not necessarily imply indoctrination. In Chapter 6 we will refer to this point again.

Finally there is the aspect of interdisciplinarity. Some educationalists use this to defend the thesis that technology should never be taught and learnt as a separate subject or course. But this does not do justice to the fact that technological knowledge is of a distinct kind and that there are well-established engineering disciplines. The fact that technological developments require the use of knowledge from various disciplines clearly calls for teaching and learning about technology in coherence and co-operation with teaching and learning about other subjects. In primary education there is not much separation between different disciplines. Teaching and learning is a holistic process here. In secondary education there is a clearer boundary between various disciplines and here co-operation between school subjects is necessary to guarantee that technological knowledge is not taught in isolation from other kinds of knowledge. In tertiary education teaching and learning about technology is highly specialized. But there is a clear tendency to have social ingredients in engineering programs. Future engineers should not only have knowledge of the technical aspects of their field, but also of the non-technical (human, social, economic) aspects. Often project work is used for the integration of the technical and non-technical aspects.

Chapter 4

TECHNOLOGICAL PROCESSES

Technology means activities. This can easily be derived from the fact that technology is in constant development. If technology were a static thing, it would not have activities as a characteristic. But what kind of activities and processes do we find in technology? Children probably would at first think of making things. Research has shown that they have more difficulties to associate technology with designing things. But in the philosophy of technology there is no discussion about both being essential activities in technology. Furthermore there is the use of technology. And use also comprises: appreciation and assessment. How can these activities be characterized? And is all designing and making technology? Or are only specific kinds of designing and making technological in nature? Such questions will be the focus for this chapter on technological processes.

1.   DESIGN PROCESSES

In general technological processes can be *design* processes, *making* processes and processes in the phase of *using and assessing* technology. For reflecting on design processes a discipline of its own right emerged, namely *design methodology*. The basis for this discipline was not always philosophical reflection, but often practitioners reflecting about their own practice and that of others. But gradually the interest for philosophy gained field in design methodology. Nigel Cross, one of the better-known design methodologists, described how the field of design methodology developed and how different ways of thinking about design processes emerged in the course of time.

In particular in the early years of design methodology there was an expectation that all design processes could be guided by one common *prescription*. With such a prescription all designers could work, irrespective of what they were designing, whether it is a house, a jumbo jet, or a nuclear power plant. Such a prescription would basically consist of three phases: analysis, synthesis and evaluation. In the phase of analysis the design problem is analyzed. This phase results in a list of requirements. In the phase of synthesis solutions for the design problem are proposed, preferably more than one solution so that a choice can be made to find an optimal solution. In the phase of evaluation the chosen design is assessed against the criteria as stated in the list of requirements. These basic phases were elaborated into an enormous variety of flowchart presentations of ideal design processes. Some of those even gained the status of technical norm (for example, in the German DIN system). Some of those schemes were linear and based on the idea that the phases were to be carried out one after the other. Other schemes had feedback loops in which there was room for backward and forward movements through the flowcharts. Again other schemes put emphasis on the decision points in the design process, or on the forms in which the information was to be found in each phase, or on the outcome of each phase. Although this made the various schemes look quite different from each other, the basic triplet of analysis, synthesis and evaluation could easily be recognized in them. Also in this vein lots of design methods and tools were developed. Some of these were fairly structured, such as the method of *morphology*, in which first the main functions of the design had to be described, then for each function a variety of solutions had to be listed, and then each combination of partial solutions was to be considered an optional solution to the overall problem. Other methods were less structured, such as the *synectic* methods that aim at taking the designers' minds to totally different contexts in the hope that this will create opportunities for coming up with revolutionary novel ideas. As for the overall flowchart schemes for design processes, here too the expectation was that such methods could be used irrespective of what was to be designed.

But as time went on, it became evident that it was too simplistic to expect all design processes to fit with this approach. Awareness grew that designing a car after all might not be quite the same as designing a new integrated circuit. Design methodologists realized that it might be worthwhile to consider what it was that caused one design problem to be different from another before prescribing one common flowchart for both processes. In other words, a *description* of the type of design problem would have to be made before coming up with a prescription for the process of solving it. Several variables appeared to be relevant in that respect, such as the extent to which the problem statement left open in what directions solutions were to be sought, the extent to which standard design tools are available, the extent to which a designer has to supplement new design requirements that are not in the problem statement but yet are necessary to consider when solving the problem. Also it became evident that design problems are different from scientific problems in that design problems generally are much less well defined. A scientific problem often can be described as finding the relationship between two or more variables. Solving that problem may not be easy at all, but it is clear what the challenge is. In design problems this is often less clear. For that reasons design problems were sometimes called 'wicked' problems. A more formal term for this is to say that design problems are *underdetermined*.

A next development in design methodology was the emerging interest in *observation* of what designers actually do when working on design problems. Various methods were used for that. Participatory observation was a very direct one: the design methodologist would then be part of the design team and observe what happened. A less direct way of observation was to take the designer out of his or her normal context and put him or her in a laboratory situation. The designer would then solve an 'artificial' design problem while saying what (s)he was thinking. Written protocols of that thinking aloud process could then be analyzed. Again another way of observing design processes was to interview the designer, once the process had been completed. Then a reconstruction of the design process could be made, based on the answers the designer had given. If well documented the design process could even be reconstructed much later, based on the minutes of design team meetings in which decisions and their arguments were described. Whichever the observation method, interesting facts were found. Designers appeared to be not so inclined to follow the design flowcharts step-by-step. They were often much more anarchistic in their design behavior. On the other hand they were more conservative with respect to the scope of solutions. Revolutionary new ideas, perhaps evoked by a synectic method, were often though of as nice for a bit of recreation, but not to be taken too seriously when it came to decisions about the design. After all, one knew what one had, and one never knew what would happen when dramatic deviations from the normal situation were opted for. Another observation was that designers do not analyze design problems 'out of the blue'. Often they first looked for a similar problem of which they already knew what the important variables were and what conditions had to be met. The term 'conjecture' was used to characterize that step. This term was borrowed from Karl Popper's 'Conjecture and Refutation' approach in the philosophy of science. In summary: observation showed that a lot of assumptions on which prescriptions were based, appeared not to be correct. Design processes were much more complex that had been imagined originally.

This caused another approach in design methodology, namely *reflection* on the complexity of the design process that is caused by the fact that design takes place in many contexts simultaneously. A designer often is part of a design team (maybe with a variety of disciplines and previous experiences represented in it), the team may be part of a company division, the division exists in the context of the whole company, and the company has to operate in the context of society. All these contexts have an impact on the designers' work. For that reason the designers have to take into account a large variety of aspects, such as functionality, safety, effects on the natural environment, costs, maintenance, patents, user friendliness, company strategies and policies, and so on. New methods and tools were developed to cope with this variety of factors. Sometimes the tendency to apply these without taking into account the nature of the design problem recurred and this resulted in simplistic approaches to the use of such methods, and also to their failure when the specific design problem and the method or tool appeared not to go together well. The need to reflect not only on the design processes as a whole, but also on the methods to be used within such processes and on the assumptions on which such methods and tools are based, again became clear.

To illustrate the need for critical reflection on design methods, the example of Quality Function will be used here. Quality Function Deployment is one of the many methods that can be seen as part of what is generally called *Total Quality Management* (TQM). In TQM the meaning of the word 'quality' is not limited to checking products at the end of the production line to inspect the number of ill-functioning products. Quality in TQM has a wider meaning. Anything that pleases the customer can be regarded as part of quality. Preventing that this customer buys an ill-functioning product of course is an element in that concept. But there is much more. It also pleases the customer when the product has exactly the functions that the customer desires, when it is simple to operate and to maintain, when it can be bought at many places, when it is nicely priced, when it can easily be disposed of when it no longer can be repaired, when it does not cause unnecessary damage to the natural environment, etcetera. In short: when the whole lifecycle of the product is pleasing to the customer. That even includes phases that the customer never gets to see, such as the manufacturing phase. If manufacturing can be cheaper because of sophisticated ways of manipulating the materials and energy, the price can be decreased and the customer will appreciate that. The emergence of such a wide scope on the consequences of design decisions fits well with reflection as an activity in the development in design methodology.

A variety of methods have been developed to see which the possible consequences of customers' wishes for each of the phases in the *lifecycle* are. This has resulted in a large series of methods that have been named *Design for X*, whereby X can be any aspect of the lifecycle. Thus we have: design for manufacturing, design for assembly, design for logistics, design for ergonomics, design for cost, design for maintenance, and design for recycling. A number of methods specifically deal with transforming the customers' desires into technical properties of the product. In a method called *Value Analysis* a survey is made of what each part of the product costs, what functions it fulfils, and what the customer is prepared to pay for those functions. If a part costs more than what its functions are worth in the eyes of the customer, the designer can consider to remove it or to integrate it into other parts to make it cheaper. Another method that aims at transforming customer requirements into technical qualities is *Quality Function Deployment*. Originally the idea was that quality could be expressed in terms of a mathematical function, in which the technical features of the product could be used as variables in a mathematical formula, the outcome of which calculation would then be a number representing the quality. Soon after the introduction of the method, this idea appeared to be too optimistic and a more subtle way of transforming customer requirements into technical features had to be developed. Nowadays the method works with matrices in which the rows represent the customer requirements and the columns represent the technical parameters. For each customer requirement a level of relationship with each of the technical parameters is identified. Those technical parameters that are most strongly related to the most important customer requirements must get priority for the designer to be given their 'ideal' value ('ideal' with respect to what the customer wants). Many companies introduced this method in their design process only to find out that it did not work. Methodological studies have shown that in many cases not the method was to be blamed for this, but the fact that the company had not reflected on the assumptions that are inbuilt in the method with respect to the company and its relationship with its customers. It makes no sense to ask customers what they want if the product is totally unknown to them. Even deeper rooted is the problem of identifying the real customer. A coach producing company is faced with a very complex customer: the tourist who will be transported in the coach, but also the touring car operator, the owner of the coach, the driver, the garage where it is to be maintained, and so on. All of these parties have their own desires, and many of them conflict. Who is to be regarded the primary customer? That is a question that needs careful reflection before applying the method in this case. In general all steps in the method assume that information is available that is necessary to make this step properly. If this is not the case, the method is bound to fail. This holds for all design methods in general: critical reflection on their assumptions is necessary to avoid improper use of those methods.

It would not be correct to suggest that prescription, description, observation and reflection are phases in the development of design methodology in the sense that each phase ended at the start of the next. Still today different types of studying design processes can be found. Roughly speaking they can be divided into two kinds: *rational problem solving* and *reflective practice*. In the first 'paradigm' the designer is seen as an information processor and the design process is very much knowledge driven. In the second 'paradigm' the designer is seen as a person who constructs his or her own reality and the process is more art-driven than knowledge-driven. Which paradigm is to be used depends on several factors, two of which are the personality of the designer (some designers feel more comfortable when working in a systematic and rational way; others feel better when working in a more loose and artistic way), and the engineering domain (architects in general design in a different way than mechanical engineers do).

In reflecting on design processes, design methodologists more and more became aware of the complexity of design problems because of the many influencing factors. In order to get some grips on these factors, it is useful to try to make a survey of the various types of factors that determine the success or failure of a product. Analysis of case studies has shown that at least the following factors are to be taken into account:
- *scientific* factors. These are the natural phenomena on which the functioning of the product is based, and of which engineers to a certain extent have knowledge;
- *technological* factors. These are the materials and processes that are available to the engineers to realize their designs;
- *market* factors. These are the ideas that customers have about the product. Mark that market factors is more than the quantitative aspects of the market that marketers usually focus on (numbers of people of certain ages and income). Aesthetical aspects are a kind of market factor also;
- *political* factors. These are the ideas that politicians have and that can be relevant to the product;
- *juridical* factors: legislation, but also existing patents that have to be taken into account;

- *ethical* factors. Although often these have been transformed into one of the other types of factors (for example when customers will refuse polluting products because of ethical considerations) engineers themselves have their ethical concerns too.

An example can illustrate this. When designing a house, an architect is confronted with all these types of factors:
- the scientific factors are in the forces that work on the house and that can be analyzed by means of classical mechanics;
- the technological factors are the construction methods that can be used to build the house. An architect has to work within the limits of the methods that are available and should not design a construction that can not be built;
- market factors are the desires and features of the customer. In the description of the QFD method it has already been pointed out that the term 'customer' can mean many things. This is the case here too. The customer can be the commissioner, but also the future inhabitants and the contractor;
- political factors in this case can be things like a city plan in which all sorts of conditions for houses to be built in certain parts of a city have been defined;
- juridical factors can be regulations concerning safety (burglars, fire), environmental effects of materials in the building, and in case the architect uses very innovative techniques possibly an existing patent;
- ethical factors: even when not required by political or juridical factors, the architect can have his or her own concerns about the effects of the house on the natural environment, safety considerations, or considerations on the issue of how the house can contribute to the well-being of the inhabitants.

The success of the design is related to the extent to which the designer has been able to make a fit between the design and these factors. Good designs fit well with the totality of these factors. Making that fit is what makes design such a complex and challenging activity.

Particularly in cases where the design process takes a long time, let us say several years, the designer is confronted with the phenomenon that most times the factors involved are not static but dynamic. New phenomena may be discovered, new technologies may become available, customers' ideas about what is beautiful and what is not may change over time, policy mat change when a new government is installed, new legislation may forbid the use of materials that before were allowed, and new ethical discussions may arise when a new technology emerges. Because of this dynamics in the factors, designers not only have to deal with the complexity of these factors but also with time as a factor. The consequence of this can be that the direction of development may change when the factors change. This not only concerns the way the design goals are to be met, but also the design goals themselves. This can be illustrated by the story of hot air engines.

Originally hot air engines were designed for niche markets, such as energy sources for water pumps. The reason for this was that in the early years of these engines there was no material that could resist a combination of high temperature and high pressure. Only with this combination high power could be realized. In terms of the factors one could say that the lack of a suitable material (a technological factor) put limits to the markets that could be served (a market factor). Besides that in the early years thermodynamics was still in its infancy and there was no proper account of what happened with the hot air in the engine (a scientific factor). But as time went on, steal became available (a change in the technological factors), and new markets emerged (for example, in the late-1930s, the Philips company in the Netherlands was looking for a quiet and electricity-independent energy source for radio sets in developing countries and found the hot air engine to be a potential solution for this). This caused a shift in the goals for designing hot air engines: rather than working on engines for very specific applications such as water pumps, engineers now tried to make the hot air engine suitable as a replacement for electricity. But again changes in the context of the hot air engine design took place. The invention of the transistor (a new technological factor) reduced the energy need of many electrical appliances and a simple battery would do as an energy source. Philips designers from that drew the conclusion that a new goal had to be set for designing hot air engines, namely for application in cars (as engines replacing the combustion engine). But once this goal was almost realized in a co-operation with the General Electric company, a new political factor emerged: in the USA the clean air act was accepted and consequently General Electric abandoned all hot air engine activities because now their first priority was to make sure that the existing (combustion) engines would meet the requirements of the new law. Together with the Ford company, Philips now defined a new goal for the hot air engine development, namely as an environment-friendly engine, and they were able to acquire government subsidies for that. The work was abandoned when it appeared that it was not possible to reconcile the conflict between the environmental qualities of the engine and the high costs, which seriously hampered competition with the combustion engine. More recently again a shift of goals can be seen: work on hot air engines now again focuses on small-scale applications, such as an energy source for central heating in houses.

What the story shows is that in the case of the hot air engine, the path towards success was not a matter of setting goals initially and then working towards those goals continuously. Rather the path is discontinuous and new goals have to be set because of changes in the context factors. A suitable term to characterize such a part could be: *piecemeal rationality*. It is rationality, because decisions are based on rational analyses of the context factors, but a piecemeal rationality because the direction of development has to be adapted to the change on context factors. It is not only the changes in factors that set limits to the role of rationality in technological developments. In such developments, as well as in scientific developments, there can be some luck involved. To indicate that this is not just sheer luck, we use the term *serendipity*. Even if one accidentally finds something, it requires a certain degree of expertise to recognize its potential for the design work that one is involved in. An example of serendipity in design is the way the famous Post-it papers were developed. A 3M engineer accidentally had developed a new type of glue that would stick only temporarily. Papers glued with it could easily be removed again. This was a matter of luck, but it would never have led to the exploitation of the glue without the expertise of the engineer who recognized that this type of glue could have entirely new applications. Another example is the invention of Local Oxidation of Silicon at Philips. A researcher accidentally found that a layer of silicon nitride protected a silicon substrate from oxidizing when the substrate was heated. He realized that silicon nitride could thus be used as a mask in the process of making integrated circuits. The resulting LOCOS process for a long time became the standard process in preparing integrated circuits and all that had started with an accidental event, but in combination with the expertise to recognize the potential of it.

Another observation with respect to the dynamics of the factors involved in technological developments is that the interaction between these factors is not the same for all products. Reflection on this dynamics can help us to identify certain patterns that enable us to distinguish between different types of technologies. These types can be defined in different ways. Designers usually work with rather classical classifications such as mechanical technologies, electrical technologies, chemical technologies, and biotechnologies, but this classification is very limited in revealing the nature of the various technologies. A classification that shows more of the different interaction patterns in the factor dynamics is the following:

- *experience-based technologies.* These are technologies in which the previous experiences of the designer are the basis for design activities. In this type of technology scientific knowledge is the result of systematically collecting these experiences and mathematizing them without searching for deeper explanations. In this type of technology social factor (market, political, juridical and ethical) factors play a role from the very start, because both designers and users have experience with the nature of the product;
- *macro-technologies.* These are technologies in which more fundamental scientific knowledge is used, but knowledge about phenomena at macro level (not at molecular level). The usual pattern here is an interaction between scientific and technological factors. For example: the invention of the steam engine (a technological development) made engineers call for knowledge about what exactly happened with the steam in the engine and this resulted in the emergence of classical thermodynamics (a scientific development); the availability of this new knowledge enabled engineers to improve the engines (a technological development), which again made engineers desire further scientific knowledge in the hope for new technological improvements. In this type of technology too, social factors can play a role from the beginning, though now moderated because of the role of scientific factors;
- *micro-technologies.* In this type of technology the design strongly draws from fundamental knowledge of micro-level particles and structures. The usual pattern here is that scientific knowledge is essential for the design. A classical example is the transistor. Initial experience-based efforts (copying the existing triode structure in solid state, as has been done successfully with the diode) led to a dead end. It was only after solid state physics (that was in fact still in state of development, but had matured to a certain extent) was applied that a type of transistor was made that could be miniaturized and mass-produced. Because of the novelty of both the technique and the knowledge about the phenomena underlying it, social factors cannot yet be dealt with in the early stages of development, contrary to the previous two types of technologies.

Some remarks have to be made about these types of technologies. In the first place, most products are a combination of technologies. Some parts may have been developed in an experience-based approach, other parts in a macro-technological approach, and again others in a micro-technological approach. In the second place, although the experience-based based technologies historically are the earliest and the micro-technologies the latest type, this does not mean that micro-technologies are the most sophisticated approach for today's technological design problems. There are many products for which still today an experience-based approach is the most straightforward and therefore the best approach. Still today it makes no sense to try to design a bridge on the basis of molecular analyses. In the third place, the design of a certain product may shift from one approach to another over time. Bridges were originally designed based on rules-of-thumb that had been derived from experience with many previous bridge designs, some of which were successful and others were not. But as time went on and methods of mechanical analysis became available, a more macro-technological approach was used. This transition was not an easy one. In the French 'Ecole des Ponts et des Chaussées' ('school of bridges and roads'; a 19th century institute for civil engineering education) from its initiation students learnt a combination of mathematics/mechanics and experiential lessons from existing bridge designs, but it took almost a century until there was a real connection between these two parts of the curriculum. Evidently the mathematical and mechanical knowledge had to be transformed in order to be usable for civil engineers when designing bridges (in Chapter 3 we have seen this also in our discussion of the relationship between scientific knowledge and technological knowledge).

All this shows that it makes a difference whether one designs an ashtray or a new car or a nanotechnology device. All design processes are complex, but all in a different way. This has consequences for the way different types of knowledge are related to the design process. In the chapter on technological knowledge (Chapter 3) we have seen that various types of technological knowledge can be distinguished. One of the ways of differentiating between different types of technological knowledge that has not yet been discussed because it is closely related to the design process is the distinction between *conceptual* (or declarative) and *procedural* (or strategic) knowledge. The first-mentioned type of knowledge is knowledge of data in a certain field. These data can be of a descriptive and of a prescriptive nature (knowledge of facts and theories, but also of rules and criteria). The second type of knowledge is about how to solve design problems. This distinction is not to be confused with the distinction between knowing-that and knowing how as if knowing-how would be the same as procedural knowledge. Knowing-how was characterized by the fact that it could not be expressed in propositions. Procedural knowledge at least partially can be expressed in propositions, and this happens when design procedures are prescribed in design handbooks. So the distinction between conceptual and procedural knowledge is a different one than the distinction between knowing-that and knowing-how. Conceptual knowledge evidently is specific for a technological domain. As we have seen earlier on in this chapter, the way designers solve design problems (and for this they refer to their procedural knowledge) also is different for different engineering domains. But not all of that is domain-specific. Knowing that a design problem involves a sound analysis of the problem is not domain-specific but applies to any design problem. But in order to be able to execute that analysis, designers have to refer to conceptual knowledge. It is not enough to know that analysis is necessary, and even more it is not enough that a designer knows for the specific field how such an analysis should be made, but to do the analysis conceptual knowledge of the specific domain is necessary. In other words: in solving a design problem, always the combination of procedural and conceptual knowledge is necessary. In section 5.4 we will see that this has important consequences for teaching and learning how to design.

In chapter 3 we have briefly mentioned the idea of *user plans* to conceptualize the phenomenon that users may use artifacts in a way that is different from the way designers had in mind when designing the artifact. As a counterpart of the user plan we can identify the *design plan*. We have met this concept briefly when discussing Plantinga's account of knowledge in Chapter 3. A design plan can be conceptualized as follows. A designer has the *intention* of realizing a certain new artifact that can fulfill a certain function. The designer has *beliefs* about the physical properties of such an artifact and how they could make the artifact fulfill that function. Then the designer sets up a *sequence of actions*, a plan, of which (she) believes that it will result in the artifact. The designer then has the *disposition to act* accordingly, and when no other considerations show up, (s)he will act accordingly. As we have seen in Chapter 3, such beliefs may have found justification (or warrant in Plantinga's terms) and may be called knowledge. This can be knowledge about the physical nature, knowledge about the functional nature, knowledge about the relationship between physical and functional nature, and as we have seen now, also knowledge of sequence of actions (knowledge of processes).

2.   MAKING PROCESSES

Making processes have not received much attention in the philosophy of technology. Some interesting contributions have been made by Hendrik van Riessen, a Dutch philosopher who has applied some concepts of the Dooyeweerd philosophy (see section 2.2) to the field of technology. He has pointed out that an important difference between the traditional craft-based production and the 'modern' production (whereby we have to keep in mind that he wrote this in the 1940s) is the energy transformation. In traditional production humans or animals delivered the energy needed for processing materials. In modern production energy is transformed from natural energy sources such as coal and gas into mechanical energy that drives a machine. This allows for a much larger scale of energy use. Van Riessen introduced the concept of a *technical operator* to indicate artifacts that are qualified (a typical Dooyeweerdian term) by their function of transforming energy. An engine is an example of a technical operator in that sense. Mass production became possible through this development in energy supply. Furthermore Van Riessen shows that one of the effects of mass production is that elements were produced that could be used in different applications. For example, gears can be mass-produced not for a specific application, but for use in many different possible devices. Here Van Riessen makes an interesting distinction between two situations: one in which the element has a meaning as an entity apart from the whole system (as in the case of the generally applicable gears), and one in which the element looses it's meaning when not in the context of the whole system. In the first situation the element has its own meaning, but can be encapsulated in a larger system. This is what Dooyeweerd called *encaptic interlacement*. In the second situation the element only derives its meaning from the whole system and this is what Van Riessen calls a *part-whole relationship*. That is the case for elements of a machine that have been made only for that particular machine, without which they have no meaning. Modern production technology according to Van Riessen shows a trend towards more encaptic interlacement, while traditional production has more of the part-whole relationship.

A further step is automatic production. In that case also the transformation of information becomes important. In a hand-driven drill, a human being watches the process and uses the information from his/her eyes to control the production process. In a CNC machine, the information is inserted into the computer and by transforming that information the machine can produce without further intervention of humans. So the development in production processes can be conceptualized as follows: tool production (materials transformation is done by the tool, energy transformation and information transformation are all done by humans), machine production (materials transformation and energy transformation are done by the machine, information transformation is done by humans) and automated production (materials transformation, energy transformation and information transformation are all done by the robot).

3.   USING AND ASSESSING PROCESSES

So far the use of technological products has not been given much attention in the analytical philosophy of technology. It has in the more Continentally-oriented philosophy of technology, but that will be discussed in the next Chapter, because to a large extent those reflections focus on the cultural aspects of the use of technology and on the relationship between the use of technology and the human will. If we want to describe the use of technology in a way similar to our description of technological artifacts and technological knowledge, we have to return to such concepts as agents, intentions, beliefs and actions, and this certainly will help us conceptualize the use of technology.

One approach to do this is by working with the idea of a 'user plan'. Such a plan in fact resembles the 'design plan', that we have already considered. User plans can be used to get an insight into how users make decisions about the use of technological devices. In the first place such decisions are based on the users' intentions, as we saw before in Chapter 2. But that is not all. For deciding if and how to use a technological artifact, not only intentions are involved, but also *beliefs* about the artifact. In other words: the user has certain intentions (he or she wants something to be accomplished) and believes that a certain artifact is suitable for that. The intentions and beliefs can be said to be the content of a user plan. Remember the example that was used in Chapter 2 of the lady who unwillingly baked her dog in the microwave oven. The lady had the belief that the microwave oven was a suitable device for drying wet dogs. Alas for the dog, this belief was false (the lady, of course, initially felt sorry too, but ended up with enough money to buy a whole kennel of new dogs and a store full of microwave ovens). Before I use the screwdriver to lift the tin can lid, I must have formed the belief that the screwdriver will be stiff and strong enough for that. This belief can be caused by different sources. Maybe someone told me that she had also used the same screwdriver quite satisfactory for that purpose. In that case my belief is formed by testimony. But perhaps I form my belief by careful inspection of the device. In that case my own perception is the cause of the belief. Another source of belief can be *reasoning*. If I have already before used the device for – again an accidental – function that puts more severe requirements to stiffness and strength of the screwdriver, than I can conclude that it should also be able to stand the task of opening the tin can. It may also be that I remember that I had once myself removed a tin can lid by using this very same screwdriver. So *memory* can also be a source of beliefs. In chapter 3 we have also considered beliefs and the way they are related to knowledge about the artifact. The next component of a user plan is the disposition to act according to his or her intention and beliefs. My intentions and my beliefs make we tend to act. When I believe that a certain action can help me reach my goals, I will be inclined to perform that action. This will not automatically lead to that action, because I may have other considerations that make me hesitate about performing the action. Perhaps my intention changes once I have realized the consequence of it in terms of the necessary actions to reach my goals. Perhaps I realize that my action will have other consequences as well that clash with other intentions that I hold. In summary, a user plan consists of an agent who has intentions, beliefs and develops dispositions to act.

Ideally a user will also assess the results of the execution of the user plan. This assessment can involve reflection on whether the action performed on the artifact has indeed contributed to reaching the intended goals, but it can go further. Assessment of the use of technological artifacts can also include the wider consequences such as possible effects on the natural environment. Such assessments can be made afterwards and can be used for reflection on future use of the artifact. Nowadays we realize that often effects have taken place that can not easily be undone. Damage can be caused that is difficult or even impossible to repair. Again the effects on the natural environment are a striking example in his respect. For that reason we have learnt to recognize the need to make judgments not after, but before we use the technology. If such judgments refer to a wide variety of possible effects (technical, economic, social) we speak of technology assessment. This is something that we will come back to in Chapter 6. But for now we want to focus on methods again, as we did in our discussion of design processes. In fact the same methodological considerations that we have seen then have to be taken into account when dealing with assessment methods. These too all have certain assumptions that have to be met in order to enable proper use of the method. In the case of technology assessment such methods have to do with the future. What most of the methods do is provide a factual basis for estimating future developments. In principle of course that is impossible. "Predicting is always difficult, but in particular when it is about the future", someone stated jokingly. The most cautious of these methods are the scenario methods. They do not make any claims about what the future will look like, but are limited to sketching possible futures. In philosophy the concept of *possible worlds* is used to indicate that our present world is only one of many possible worlds. Things could just as well have been otherwise, and reflecting on other possible worlds sometimes supports our reasoning. Here the term *counterfactuals* is used. If we want to reason about present situations it can be helpful to reason about alternatives. "What if . . ." such reasoning patterns could be characterized by. This is typically the type of reasoning that we find in scenario techniques. Such reasoning is supported by the use of models. *Modeling* is an activity that we find in many sciences, and also the engineering sciences make use of them. In fact, the use of models can be found throughout technological processes: in design processes, making processes and use/assessment processes. In Chapter 3 we have seen how modeling plays a role in engineering sciences.

Other technology assessments, however, do not have the limitation of only speaking about possible worlds. There are other methods that aim at making claims about what the future *will* look like rather than what it *can* look like. Here we find all sorts of forecasting methods. We all know the stories about how such methods can fail terribly to produce reliable predictions. Sometimes it seems that even a horoscope would do better than such methods. Does that mean that such methods have no value? No, that would be a wrong conclusion. As in the case of failing design methods (for instance the QFD method) often failure is not due to the method, but to improper use because of neglected assumptions in the method. Forecasting methods, like all methods, have such assumptions, in particular about the reliability of the data on which the forecasting is based. In principle such methods function on a simple basis: 'garbage in, garbage out'. The use of bad data results in bad predictions, but the problem is that the method itself does not make warnings about that. The method is as patient as a method can be and swallows all data that are inserted and without protest produces predictions, whatever their quality may be. It is the user of the method that has to reflect carefully about these issues.

4.   TEACHING AND LEARNING TECHNOLOGICAL PROCESSES

We have seen that the philosophy of technology tells us that all methods have their assumptions, and that it is important to realize what those assumptions are when applying those methods. In education this is not always done. Numerous textbooks for technology education present flowcharts that prescribe design processes, based on the assumption that they can be applied to any design project that pupils or students will do. Educational research has shown that this can lead to frustrating situations, whereby pupils and students can be forced to do things that for that particular situation so not seem to make sense, but still are prescribed in the design process flowchart. The same is true for all sorts of methods for certain parts of design processes, such as coming up with different solutions for the design problem. Of course the extent to which it can be expected that pupils themselves reflect on the methods varies with age and educational level. In the earlier years of education it is mainly the teacher that will have to think critically about the fitness of the method for the particular situation. Students in higher levels of education can be expected to be more active in that, and it is important to make them do such thinking in order to make them aware of the importance of such reflections for a proper use of methods for designing, making, using and assessing. Also it is important to make them aware of the differences between different types of technologies. In the earlier years of education it is important to help them see the difference between technology and other human activities. At that phase understanding the differences within the field of technology would be asked too much. But in the late years, students should acquire an understanding of the variation of technologies. By then such differences are important for them in case they consider opting for a technological career. They have to be aware that being a architect and being a chemical engineer may both be called 'technological professions', but there is a vast difference between those two professions. This difference is reflected in the different ways in which the architect and the chemical engineer use methods for designing, making, using and assessing products.

Chapter 5

TECHNOLOGY AND THE NATURE OF HUMANS

Technology is an activity that is intrinsic to humans. This is a claim that has been made by many philosophers. In this chapter we will explore what it means for humans to be technological beings. This chapter also differs from previous chapters in that we will now mainly draw from the cultural philosophy rather than from the analytical philosophy (in chapter 1 this distinction has been dealt with). As we will see, often the continental philosophy is much more critical about technology than the analytical one. It stimulates us to live our lives in a technological world much more consciously and critically by emphasizing the non-neutrality of technology.

1.   TECHNOLOGY AND HUMAN NEEDS AND DESIRES

Why do humans behave technologically? The most obvious answer is: because they have needs to be fulfilled. Those can be various types of needs. Abraham Maslov has presented a survey of the various types of needs humans may have. According to him there is a hierarchy of needs. At the bottom of this hierarchy we have the very basic needs to survive, such as food, water, oxygen, in other words: the physiological needs. The next level of needs in Maslow's taxonomy is the level of safety needs: security, stability, protection and the like. Next is the level of the belongingness and love needs. All humans feel the need to be loved and to love. Next are the esteem needs: we want to be respected by others. These are needs like mastery and competence, independence and freedom. The highest level of needs in Maslow's taxonomy is the level of self-actualization needs: we feel the need to express ourselves in music, literature and the like. Technological developments have to do with the fact that we try to address each of these types of needs better, but also we try to address more and more needs by technology. A similar distinction is made by Friedrich Rapp in his book 'Analytical philosophy of technology'. According to him there are three main motives for humans to develop technology: the first motive is the basic human need to survive, secondly there are motives of power and control, and thirdly there are motives related to the intellectual capacities of humans (analog to Maslov's highest level of needs). In the course of this chapter we will investigate these levels of motives.

2.   TECHNOLOGY AS AN EXTENSION OF NATURAL HUMAN ORGANS

One of the first philosophers who is generally accepted as being truly a 'philosopher of technology' is Ernst Kapp. He has pointed out that technology is the way humans extend their own natural organs. Why did humans make a fist axe? Because their hands were too weak and too blunt in order to cut wood. Why did they come up with the idea of a spear? Because their arms were too short and their legs were too slow in order to catch a running animal. Why did they invent pots to store food? Because they only had two hands on their body, and there was a lot of food to be stored. Why did they invent lenses? That was because their eyes were not capable of seeing very small things, or things that were very far away. Likewise all technical artifacts can be explained to be extensions of natural human organs, according to Kapp. At first sight this seems quite reasonable. But as technologies get more complex, it is more difficult to see in what sense they are extensions of our human organs. Let us take the Internet as an example. In a way this can be seen as an extension of our human voice, because it replaces us telling the information to each other. But the system is very complex and contains many elements that are not directly extensions of the human voice and its effects are much more than just extending the amount of shared information over larger distances. Therefore Kapp's analysis is too simplistic to serve as an adequate description of what the Internet is.

In principle there are two possible perspectives on artifacts as extensions of our human capabilities. In the first perspective, this extension is a logical next step in the evolution of mankind. In a way very similar to the emergence of new limbs in new types of living creatures in the process of evolution, technological devices emerge in a quasi-evolutionary process. Thus mankind takes the next step at the ladder of evolution. In this vision there is not much threatening in technological devices, at least not for mankind itself (maybe for other types of living creatures, because in the evolutionary process some types have become extinct because of the improved capacities of others). In the second perspective there is a fundamental change in the history of mankind. No longer do the natural extensions of man determine his ability to survive, but artificial extensions, which were designed not by the 'blind' process of evolution, but intentionally, by humans themselves. In that vision such breaking away from the natural evolutionary process can be a great threat to the natural balance in the world as a whole.

3. ARTIFACTS AS INTERMEDIARIES BETWEEN US AND OUR LIFEWORLD

One of the most famous continental philosophers, who wrote about technology, is Martin Heidegger. His philosophical ideas are concerned with the way we see and interact with our environment. On the one hand, we are part of this environment and in constant interaction with it, and on the other hand we realize that we are separate beings. These two kinds of awareness can also be seen in the way we use technical artifacts. To illustrate this, Heidegger uses the example of a hammer. When we see it lying on the table, we experience it rather as a part of our environment than as a part of our selves. But when we pick it up and start using it to hammer a nail into a piece of wood, something happens to the way we experience the hammer. It almost seems like it disappears from our consciousness and becomes part of us. We no longer see the hammer as something in our environment, but it becomes part of our being. The awareness of the hammer being a part of our environment only returns, when the hammer fails to function properly. Then we realize that we have a hammer in our hand, and we start examining at it in order to find out what is wrong with it. The transition from one kind of awareness of the hammer to the other is quite abrupt. It can be indicated as a *Gestalt* switch, this term meaning the way we experience the totality of ourselves in relation to our environment.

Heidegger in later publications expressed great concern about the way humans tend to decrease the quality of their existence by seeing their environment more and more primarily as something that must bring forth resources for practical use. Modern technology enhances that in a way that is much stronger than traditional technologies did. This threatens to turn human existence into a technological existence. In a famous interview for a German magazine, Der Zeit, Heidegger said that 'only a God can now save us', something that dramatically turns our attention to other aspects of life than the technological exploitation of our lifeworld.

Heidegger's philosophical approach is called *existentialism*. It focuses on the way we experience our existence. Related to this is *phenomenology*. In phenomenology we see our experience of reality as one total phenomenon rather than splitting it up into subjects and objects. One of Heidegger's followers, Don Ihde, has extended Heidegger's analysis of our interaction with technological artifacts into a variety of different types of Gestalt switches. Rather than reflecting on the way we see technology (as Heidegger did), Ihde has analyzed the way technological artifacts shape our view of reality. As he shows, technology plays an important part in our perception of reality. Ihde distinguishes the following types of intermediary roles of technologies in our perception of reality:

- when I look to a landscape through a window, the window has an influence on the way I perceive the landscape, because it limits my view. Partially the window disappears from my consciousness, as the hammer did in Heidegger's example, but partially I am still aware of its presence because of dust particles I can see on it, or perhaps some distortions in the glass. If the window is very transparent we can represent the situation as follows: (I-window)→world. The parentheses indicate that the window has become part of myself in my viewing the outside world. The window withdraws from my consciousness and becomes embodied in me. More generally stated the relationship is: (I-technology)→world. This is what Ihde calls an *embodiment* relation. The embodiment is even stronger in the case of my viewing the world through a pair of glasses. Again the glasses change the way I perceive the world, but they function so convincingly that I do not notice that effect. A similar effect but related to acting in the world rather than perceiving it, can be seen with experienced drivers. They know the car so well that it almost becomes part of their own body and in their moving through the world, they are hardly aware of the fact that the car is there. A third example is an experienced flute player for whom the flute has almost become part of her own body in producing the sound;
- when an operator of a power plant wants to have information about what happens inside the power plant, (s)he reads the instrument panel. It is then taken for granted that what is read from this instrument panel is so closely connected to the inside of the power plant that the two are like one totality. In that case the instrument panel as a tool for observing does not become part of my body, but of the world that I observe. The relationship can then be presented as: I→(instrument panel-world). More

generally: I→(technology-world). This is what Ihde calls a *hermeneutic* relation. What I see now needs to be interpreted (and that is what hermeneutics is all about) in order to be understood (contrary to the window and glasses example). Other examples are infrared pictures of landscapes and X-ray and MRI representations of (parts of) human bodies. Those two need interpretation to enable us to see reality;

- when I watch a movie, I am aware that what I see is not reality. The movie itself has become the reality that I perceive. There may be a true story behind the movie (i.e. the technology), but that remains entirely at the background. The relation can be characterized as: I→technology-(-world). Ihde calls this an *alterity* relation. The technology in itself is now the 'other' that I view. The parentheses now indicate that there may be, but need not be, a relation through the technology to the world;
- it may also be that not the real world remains hidden in the background, but the technology does. Think of technologies that light or heat. You do not notice the technologies (except perhaps a vague humming at the background and the relation is what Ihde calls a *background* relation: I→(technology-)-world).

Finally Ihde writes about what he calls 'horizontal phenomena, in which the distinction between the natural and the artificial starts to disappear. This happens in the case of various types of medical technologies such as implants and manipulating genetic materials.

Ihde does not only present these categories as a neutral analysis, but he also expresses concerns that if we are not sufficiently aware of the intermediary role of technologies in our interactions with reality and we get used to the reductions that technology causes in the way we experience reality, we may loose sense of how rich our existence can be. This concern has been elaborated by Albert Borgmann in his *device paradigm*. Borgmann argues that devices have become such an omnipresent part of our world that we hardly know what it is to have a direct experience with nature. Borgmann, who, like Ihde, often refers to Heidegger to positional his philosophical stance, distinguishes devices from things in that things still require our human skills to be operated, but devices de-skill us because they function almost entirely on their own. Devices dis-engage us in our relationship with the lifeworld around us. Partly this is because of the uniformity of many technologies. In earlier days, going to other countries was a rich experience because we encountered new food, new objects, and new sceneries. Nowadays we can have Chinese food at home, buy products from all over the world (and besides there are less and less products anyway that are still characteristic for a certain country or region), and we can produce all sorts of sceneries ourselves or watch them on television. There are almost no surprises left when we travel. This results in a dis-engaged relation with reality.

What remedy for this does Borgmann recommend? That can be summarized in the term *focal* things and practices. As an example Borgmann mentions running (for pleasure, not for getting the bus). Running fully engages body and mind and therefore is a remedy against being caught in the web of the dis-engagement that the devices around us try to force upon us. Another example is preparing and having a festive meal, not of pre-designed and precooked stuff, but of ingredients that are close to raw materials. This stimulates us to make our own considerations about means-ends relationships rather than leaving those to the devices with their in-built means-ends relations. Although at first sight this seems to be an attractive remedy, everyone who has tried it will soon find out that such focal activities tend to be the exceptions rather than the rule, given the dominant position of technical artifacts in our world. For other philosophers of technology, such as Andrew Feenberg and Langdon Winner, Borgmann's solution therefore is seen as insufficient and not very effective, because focal activities can hardly be expected to become the main part of our lives. Besides that they think only politics can bring a real solution for the problem. Nearly all examples that Borgmann uses to illustrate the concept of focal activities relate to leisure time activities, and not to the professional life. This may well be an indication for the limitations of the therapy he offers to be freed from the disengaging effects of devices. The effect of focal activities cannot be large as long as the overall social and political systems that support the negative effects of technology remain intact. Larry Hickman, a pragmatist philosopher, has criticized the idea that devices have this effect. According to him there are other effects as well. He uses the example of television to admit that a lot of useless television programs are a bad replacement for direct social relationships, but on the other hand educational television programs can have a strong engaging effect. In general one can question the assumption that devices nearly always impoverish our experience of reality, as Heidegger and Borgmann claim. As a pragmatist and follower of John Dewey, Hickman sees the solution for negative effects of technology not in experts' analyses, but in the learning through experimenting process of all parties involved.

The idea of the omnipresence and pervasiveness of technology in our world is certainly not new. Decades earlier, a French philosopher, Jacques Ellul, had already pointed out this important aspect of technology. He paid much attention to the system character of technology that gave a certain autonomy to technology. Technology became a self-regulating mechanism on which society had no influence. Ellul therefore sketched a very pessimistic image of the influence of technology on society and in fact he hardly saw any way out. In that respect Borgmann does not make much progress in the eyes of those who do not believe the focal activities will help a great deal because they leave the system character of technology still intact. In section 5.5 we will discuss the issue of control over or by technology in some more detail.

Another French philosopher who has reflected on the position of technological artifacts as intermediaries between the natural and the cultural world is George Simondon. According to him technological artifacts are one of the ways humans use to give value and significance to the world around them, in a similar way as they do in religion or science. Technological objects have no existence in themselves, but only in relation to the world in which they have emerged. They form a transition between the natural and the artificial or cultural world. There are three possibilities here: either they make the natural and the artificial world oppose each other (for example in the case when environmental harm is done), or they isolate the natural world (for example when a city is built underneath the earth surface), or they function because of a junction between the two worlds (for example in the case of a windmill). This analysis of course can lead to quite different appreciations of the technological artifacts in the three cases.

4. AI AND THE INTERNET

One of the technologies that most clearly show the limitations of technology-mediated experiences is the Internet. Hubert Dreyfus is a philosopher who wrote extensively about this. In particular he pointed out that the lack of bodily presence is a serious barrier for having realistic experiences with the lifeworld. The Internet allows us access to an enormous amount of information, but it also allows us to take part in communications with other persons. The use of e-mail is a simple version of that, but there are more sophisticated ones. In a MUD, a multi-user domain, several people can be connected to a virtual world in which they can live as an artificial being with an identity that to a certain extent can be created by them selves. But this community is entirely a virtual one. Dreyfus argues that the lack of bodily experience makes this a very poor experience from a humanistic point of view. The growing popularity of such virtual meetings, not only in MUDs but also in numerous other kinds of 'virtual realities' (truly a contradiction within terms!), should be a reason for concern according to Dreyfus. People start to think that this is what real life is like, and forget the much richer experiences of the past. Others have criticized this by pointing out that the coming of telephones also caused the emergence of body-less communication, but still does not seem to have deteriorated the quality of our communications (to the contrary, these people say, it has created lots of new opportunities for communication between people who otherwise would not have a chance of having contact at all). But the question remains whether the extent to which and the manner in which Internet changed the world is the same as that of the telephone. Virtual realities nowadays can be made so sophisticated that there is a very strong suggestion that it presents a real-world experience rather than a reductive one. This makes the technology much more misleading than e.g. telephone, in which the deductive character of the communication is still very obvious.

Another interesting area from the point of view of the role of technology in human experiences is *Artificial Intelligence* (AI). These technologies nowadays can be so sophisticated that we almost get the impression that the machines that we communicate with have human characteristics. This has given rise to philosophical debates about the question at which point we can say that technological objects can 'think'. Several philosophers defend the claim that today technologies exist that can be said to have the ability of thinking, similar to the human ability to think. Similarities between computer information processing and human brain information processing have already been suggested by psychologists such as Herbert Simon who made empirical studies of problem solving by humans and by computers (e.g. solving chess problems). And as even the greatest of human chess players have been defeated by computer chess programs, such philosophers feel quite confident in making the claim that computers can think just like humans can. Others, though, want to stick to their denial of this, thereby often pointing to the fact that emotions are not part of computer information processing. Speculations about the possibilities of enabling computers to have emotions also are manifold. At least the suggestion can be made that they have them. In Japan there has been a very popular toy called 'tamagochi', a sort of egg-shaped device with a display that showed a face in various moods, depending on the treatment that was given by the owner-child. The face would look happy when the tamagochi was given positive attention, it would look sad when 'punished' and it would start screaming when neglected too long, just like a neglected baby would. More sophisticated are the electronic dogs called AIBO, also originating from Japan. And indeed, the communication skills these robots have can be quite convincing. The famous Turing test was developed to prove that these skills may become so advanced that in some cases humans can no longer tell whether they have communicated with a machine or with a human being. There has been a lot of controversy over this test and many people nowadays no longer accept it as a valid test to distinguish between human and machine intelligence.

Moviemakers have gratefully grabbed their chances and used wonderful opportunities to visualize the almost boundless new possibilities that information technologies seem to offer in terms of computers having thinking skills and even emotions. The movie Artificial Intelligence by Steven Spielberg is an example of that. An artificial boy searches for true love from his human 'parents' even long after they have died. HAL, the computer that controls a space station in the year 2001 in the classic movie based on the novel '2001, A Space Odyssey' by Clarke, starts to mistrust his human inhabitants and even starts to kill them. In both cases a technological artifact is ascribed emotional capacities.

Again the question can be asked what the quality of life is when we take human-computer interactions for granted as a replacement of human-human communications, and start thinking that this is what life has to offer. Would not replacing human-human contacts by human-computer interaction be a pretty poor way of life? That is certainly what a number of philosophers say. And here again the rapidly increasing popularity of such technologies causes them to worry.

5. CONTROLLING TECHNOLOGY OR BEING CONTROLLED BY TECHNOLOGY

The issue of having control over technology versus being controlled by technology remained an important one throughout the development of the philosophy of technology (in particular in the Continental tradition). It revives each time a technology with possible strong effects emerges. In the previous century cybernetics was the technology that most prominently promoted the idea of control by technology. Norbert Wiener became well known for his writings in which he expressed the need to have technological control over society in order to solve its problems. Another philosopher in the previous century who expressed great expectation from technological control for solving social problems was Karl Marx. In his view technology was important to realize the transition from a capitalist to a communist society. Three more contemporary examples of technologies that have a potential for acquiring a far-reaching control over society, even though their developers certainly do not promote this as such, like Wiener, Marx and others did, are: bioengineering, ambient technology, and nanotechnology.

Bioengineering is expected to have far-reaching consequences. It is related to the fundamentals of life. Through bioengineering genetic properties can be manipulated and this will have an impact on all future generations. Because of the yet largely unknown effects, the fear that bioengineering can become a power that overrules us is not unjustified, in spite of all the comforting words of experts. Even apart from the ethical question whether or not human beings should manipulate the foundations of life (see Chapter 6 for that discussion), the uncertainties in the effects of bioengineering are a reason for caution, as is recognized by e.g. international agencies.

Another intriguing development is called *ambient technology*. This term refers to the fact that more and more technologies in the home are hidden so that we do not have to bother with a complex switch panel. By observing our habits and preferences the house will gradually adapt the functioning of the hidden technologies in order to make it fit with what it perceives as our needs. At first sight, that may seem to be an advantage. But after a while one realizes that the house, once it has determined the functioning of the technologies, then will start manipulating us. After the house has observed that we tend to rise at about 7 am and drink coffee at 8 am before we leave, it will start switching on the coffee machine at around 7.45 am so that there is coffee available at 8 am. But from then on we will either have to drink coffee at 7.45 or throw away the coffee when we don't feel like having coffee that morning. And of course we don't like to throw away that coffee so for the sake of its availability we will drink it, even when we would not have made it if we could have decided about making the coffee ourselves. Do we control the house or does the house control us? That becomes an interesting question.

A third example of a new technological development for which the issue of control seems to become relevant is the field of *nanotechnologies*. Some of those are already daily practice, such as very thin coatings on glasses with a thickness of only few atoms. 'Nano' (from the Greek word for 'dwarf') refers to nanometer, the size of an atom. Nanotechnology in its extreme form aims at manipulating individual atoms (this is called molecular nanotechnology). A lot of that is still fantasy, but some people, such as Eric Drexler, have written futurological reflections in which independent devices (the universal assemblers) construct other devices by manipulating individual molecules. Already now the dangers of such devices have been identified, and again perhaps most impressively by artists. The novel 'Prey' by Michael Crichton describes the escape of a set of independent tiny robots that become a great danger to humans because they can break them down molecule by molecule without any possibility of being stopped by other humans. Although the term nanotechnology is used nowhere in the novel, critics have recognized that there is a strong similarity with this new type of technology and that the authors aim was no other than making us aware of the possible dangers of nanotechnology.

What makes people worry about these technologies is the fact that they are so sophisticated that it is hard to see how they can be controlled. Either they are related to the manipulation of the fundamentals of life (genetic material or even the individual molecules) or they are so well hidden and so advanced in their actions on us that we feel that we are loosing control over these developments and fear that Ellul's dark prophesies may become reality particularly in such cases.

The total control over technology over society has been visualized wonderfully by, again, moviemakers. Some of these movies have become true classics. An example of that is the movie Metropolis that offers a horrible view on a future in which human slaves work in an underground environment in which machines totally determine their work. In fact this movie extends and intensifies the perspective that was already offered in an even more 'classical' movie: Modern Times, by Charles Chaplin. This movie refers to the mass production lines in which humans almost entirely become part of the technological system.

6. THE SOCIAL AND POLITICAL DIMENSION OF TECHNICAL ARTIFACTS

As we saw in section 5.5, Ellul has suggested that the relationship between technology and society is mainly a one-way influence: technology dominates social life, and not the other way round. Other philosophers have pointed out, though, that there is also an influence the other way round. Technology is not just a natural process that necessarily happens and on which we have no influence. To the contrary, technology is totally a human-originated phenomenon and therefore we have full control over it. The problem is not that we cannot control technology, but that we leave it to certain social parties, such as the engineers. Those parties often suggest that the way they develop and implement technology is the best, and perhaps even the only one that is possible, but when others would be keener on analyzing and criticizing their views, a much more balanced control over technology would emerge.

Feenberg in one of his books described a wonderful example of this, namely the development of the Minitel information technology in France. According to him, top-down development of technology is typical for France and the Minitel idea is an example of that. Minitel was meant to be a computerized information source for French citizens, not unlike Teletext in other countries. Each family was given a terminal to allow the people access to the information system. But soon some sophisticated users found out that it was possible to hack the system and start exchanging other information that was not provided by the government. Their way of using the system in a relatively short time became popular among the whole French population. Thus the users turned the Minitel system into a kind of Internet 'avant-la-lettre'. Feenberg promotes this almost anarchistic behavior of users as an alternative to the servile attitude of most people towards technology that caused philosophers like Ellul to describe technology as an autonomous system.

Langdon Winner more or less has the same message. He discusses the political dimension of technical artifacts. Technology is never neutral but has a large impact on our lives. Therefore the role of technology in society should be the outcome of a truly democratic political process. For him decentralization of technology will be a positive result of such a process. The problem he sees, though, is how to get all relevant parties involved in this process. Like Feenberg, his approach is more in the tradition of a group of philosophers that are called the Frankfurter Schule, and in which we find names like Jürgen Habermas en Theodor Adorno (see also section 5.9). Winner, though, does not want to position himself in that stream. Generally speaking, the examples he uses in his publications are more pessimistic than Feenberg's examples. Winner emphasizes that technology can be used by politicians to maintain a certain political situation, whereas Feenberg showed that users can overtake technology to make it serve their own purposes.

In the Social Construction Of Technology (SCOT) perspective, there is a very strong emphasis on the influence of social actors on technological developments. In this view technical factors almost play no role in technological developments. The example that has become almost a 'classic' one is the bicycle, as described in its development by Wybe Bijker. According to Bijker the whole development of the bicycle is a matter of how people perceived this product. Initially it was not seen as a transportation means, but rather as a device with which young men could show their braveness and skills to young ladies to impress them. In that time the bike was a sort of 'macho machine', and the design of the bike was according to this idea: one very big and one very small wheel so that riding the bike would require extreme capabilities. Later the bike was seen as a transportation means primarily, first for ladies, and later also for men. That was what caused the changes in the design (two equally-sized wheels and various new parts to ensure safe riding), again according to Bijker.

One consequence of this social orientation on technological developments is that one could use political decisions to take away decisions about the use of technology from the user and let them be built into the artifact. That could be a solution to problems where it is known or can be expected that a large majority of users will not behave in a responsible way. An example of this is the behavior of car drivers. Even though the law forbids driving faster than the speed limit, and obliges to use the safety belt, it is well known that many car drivers do not keep those rules. In such a case a government could decide to make a law that states that all cars should be designed in such a way that the driver simply can not drive faster than the speed limit because the car does not enable that. Likewise a law can be made that all cars are designed in such a way that the car simply will not start until the driver has put on the safety belt. The responsibility for driving safely in such cases is taken away from the driver and transferred to the car. Of course such an approach would be the cause of lots of social debates, because it would enhance the idea that humans are controlled by technology rather than having control over it.

7. POSTMODERN TECHNOLOGIES

In a way, the SCOT vision on technology can also be found in postmodern visions on technology. Here too, technology is what it is due to what we think it is. But contrary to the SCOT vision, postmodernists focus on the individual rather than on social groups. Each of us has his or her own feelings about technology, and therefore we all have our own perspective on what technology is, and on what good or bad technology is. Postmodernism is based on the assumption that there is no single truth (or 'big story' in the terms of Lyotard, one of the best-known postmodern authors), but only a variety of individual truths ('small stories' in Lyotard's terminology). Related to this is the blurring of boundaries that previously people saw as absolute. Not only truth becomes relative, but also traditional categories, such as biological versus mechanical beings. An example of this is Donna Haraway's appreciation for the concept of Cyborgs (in her 'Cyborg manifesto'): beings that are human and robot at the same time. Again referring to movies, we can see Robocop and Terminator as such. And this is not only science fiction. By now medical technologies have advanced to such an extent that we can replace almost every par of a human body by an artificial part. How far must one go in replacing human body parts by artificial ones before the human has been turned into a robot? Also the boundary between life and death has been blurred by our increased capacities to keep a human body that normally would have been declared to be 'dead' 'alive' by means of a whole set of machines that take over functions that the human body is no longer capable of realizing by itself.

One of the first technological domains where the ideas of postmodernism were practiced is *architecture*. Postmodern architecture has done away with the idea that there should be consistence of style within a building. Postmodern architects see no problem in creating a building that has Roman, Gothic, functionalist and whatever other architectural styles all combined in one and the same construction.

Another technological field with postmodern characteristics is the *Internet*. Here we see the idea that there is no single truth and that there can be various, perhaps even conflicting truths living together in the same environment. The information on Internet is not filtered in any way. Distinguishing between truth and non-truth is almost impossible. Educationalists should notice this when they give assignments to pupils in which they have to collect information from the Internet. Pupils then will take every information they find to be true and reliable. This attitude is enhanced by the medium that in no way stimulates to seek to distinguish between truth and non-truth. Internet also shows traces of the blurring boundaries: often Internet presentations are so convincing that the traditional boundary between reality and virtuality has almost disappeared. The virtual reality of Internet seems to have become a reality of its own. Here too, we will find young people most sensitive to this suggestion.

The possibility of creating a virtual reality that is so convincing that it can make us confuse reality and virtuality is another theme that movie makers have used to create intriguing movies. The Matrix trilogy is maybe the best-known example of that. In this movie what we experience as 'normal life' appears to be a computer program in which we are caught without knowing it. The theme of the movie is about being freed from this illusion and finding the real life. This strongly reminds of Plato's cave analogy. Plato in one of his writings claims that what we experience as 'real life' in fact is but a vague shadow of the ideal world that he considers being the real world. It is the philosopher that escapes from the cave world and discovers that there is an outside world. The philosopher's task then becomes to go back into the cave and try to convince the other people that they are locked up in the cave and need to free them selves. This is just one of the many philosophies that The Matrix seems to refer to, and as a result many philosophical books and articles have already been written about this movie, so of which by well-known philosophers. Two other movies that deal with the theme of reality versus virtuality are Simone and The Truman Show. In the first-mentioned movie a film producer uses software given to him by a friend to create a virtual female movie star and inserts her in his new movies. The public is convinced that she is a real person and the film producer constantly has to find ways of concealing her virtuality against people that want to meet her in person. In The Truman Show the main character of the movie at a certain moment finds out that what he experiences as his own normal life is not reality. His life appears to be a movie in which he is the main character. As soon as he knows this he seeks to 'escape' from this movie existence to enter 'real life'.

The postmodern philosophy is very popular today, even though maybe most followers will not be sufficiently acquainted with philosophy to name their view as such. On the other hand there are people for whom it is not acceptable to think that all truth is relative, because they believe in one truth that holds for all places and all times. Christians can be an example of this, although many of them in their lifestyle no doubt display postmodern characteristics.

8.   TOWARDS NEW LIFESTYLES

In the previous sections some remedies for overcoming the dominance of technology over humans and society have been mentioned already, but for some philosophers and others these are not radical enough. Probably the most radical response to an emerging technology was that of the Luddites. They completely rejected technology and even fought it (by destroying the steam engines that they considered to be a great threat to human freedom). But as we all know, they lost the battle and the steam engine has already long ago been surpassed by technologies that have an even much larger effect on the use of energy in society. A more subtle way of resisting against being controlled by technology can be found in certain Amish groups. The popular view on the Amish is that they are people that resist against all new technologies and live like in the Middle-Ages. But that image is not correct. The Amish do accept certain new technologies, but only on certain conditions. Those technologies that have a tendency to dominate our lives and bring us in too close contact with the outside world are rejected and those technologies, for which one can always decide whether or not to use them and thus remain in isolation from the outside world, are accepted. Television is generally not accepted by them, because it brings them in too close contact with the world. Telephone is often accepted because they can enhance contacts within the community, but not in the homes, where they can constantly force us to answer the phone. Phones are put in shared locations where people can go to make a phone call, but are not disturbed by incoming calls. Some time ago a newspaper reported claimed that he had 'caught' an Amish man 'in the act' when he was using a mobile phone. This reported had clearly not understood that mobile phones fit perfectly well with the Amish criteria for acceptable technologies: one can turn it on to make a phone call and turn it of in order not to be forced to answer. The example shows that the Amish have nothing against modern technologies as such, but only when they become dominant and make us dependant on what they see as the outside world. Another example of this is energy production: the Amish have electricity, but generate it locally. In that way they are not connected with, and therefore not dependant on centralized energy supply. It should be remarked that some Amish groups reject more technologies than other groups. This depends on the expectations they have of the possible effects of new technologies. While appreciating their attitude to be selective in the use of technology rather than first letting technology in and afterwards trying to control it, as is often the case in most of our societies today, it should be admitted that they often reject technologies too quickly because they overestimate the possible negative effects of those technologies. That is probably why they generally but incorrectly have the reputation of being technology haters.

Another group of people that shows great consciousness in using technology in a way that fits their religious basis are the orthodox Jews. When visiting Israel it is interesting to observe how numerous technologies have been adapted according to the needs of the orthodox Jewish religion. One of the most important issues in Jewish religion is the day of rest, the Sabbath. Orthodox Jews have certain interpretations of what it means not to work. One of those interpretations is that making fire is doing work. That causes a lot of problems with electrical appliances, because the spark that is created when we use a switch is considered to be a fire that one makes, and therefore the Sabbath rule forbids the use of electrical switches. One of the consequences of that is that one is not allowed to push any button when using an elevator on Sabbath. But rather than avoiding the use of the elevator and walking all the way up to the tenth floor of a hotel, people have invented the Sabbath elevator: on Sabbath the elevator is programmed to make stops at all floors. Admitted, that makes the trip to the tenth floor more time-consuming than on other days, but one can make the trip without breaking the rule of not making fire on the Sabbath. Heating, of course, is also problematic on Sabbath. This has caused people to come up with creative ideas for meals that can be prepared the day before Sabbath and kept hot in thermos jugs or pots, so that they can be consumed on Sabbath reasonably warm but without being heated that day. Coffee on Sabbath is not made with a coffee machine, but with hot water (heated the day before and kept in a thermos jug) and instant coffee powder. So both modern technologies (elevator automation) and traditional technologies (for keeping things warm) are used to make technological appliances fit with the conditions of the orthodox Jewish religion.

A Dutch philosopher, who has issued warnings about the danger of technology controlling us rather than us controlling technology and promoted a lifestyle that focuses on not being controlled by technology, is Egbert Schuurman. His analysis goes beyond the level of only deciding whether or not to accept a technology, but also deals with the development of new technologies. He has shown that there are different motives for developing technology. Since the Enlightenment, the *motive of having power* has been an important motive, both for science and for technology. This can be illustrated by Francis Bacon's adagium: knowledge is power. It has led to humans seeing reality only as a resource that can be used 'ad libitum'. The results are clear: depletion of materials and energy sources, pollution and disturbance of landscapes. Furthermore, the desire to control by technology has often had the reverse effect: technology became such a dominating force that humans felt controlled by it. This is what can be called the dialectics of Enlightenment: humans seek to have power and control over reality, but in the end appear to be controlled by technology. Schuurman sees the only way out in the replacement of the motive of control by the *motive of love and care* (or in terms that have been derived from the Bible: stewardship and service to God and humans). It is clear that Schuurman's critique on much of our current culture (for which he often uses the term 'Babylon culture' because of the power motive that drove people o build the tower of Babylon in the Bible book Genesis) is quite different from the critique of Heidegger and the contemporary philosophers of technology that were inspired by him (such as Ihde and Borgmann). For them the main problem is in the way people experience reality; for Schuurman it is in the motives for doing what the do.

9.   CONTINUING INFLUENCES FROM THE PHILOSOPHICAL PAST

Now that we have seen various philosophers of technology and their ideas about men and technology, we can recognize that there are certain philosophical streams that most of these philosophers can be characterized by. Four of these streams are:

* phenomenology and existentialism; this stream is generally seen to have Husserl and Heidegger as important 'fathers'. Today we find philosophers of technology such as Don Ihde and Albert Borgmann (see section 5.3) clearly seeking their roots in that tradition. They focus on the way individuals experience reality, and generally they see dangers in the way technology can impoverish those experiences;
* followers of the Frankfurter Schule; this 'school' of philosophy has various 'fathers' too: Horkheimer, Adorno, Marcuse and Habermas. Today philosophers like Andrew Feenberg and Langdon Winner (see section 5.6) see their inspirations in this line of thinking, in which the social and political aspects are seen as primary driving forces behind changes in reality; these philosophers also see dangers in technology but have high expectations of the possibilities to influence technology by political means;
* pragmatists; here the name of John Dewey can be mentioned as one of the 'fathers' of this tradition; today we find Larry Hickman (see section 5.3) developing a philosophy of technology in that line of thinking. Briefly stated one can say that in this line of thinking whatever is useful is true;
* postmodernists; here we find for example François Lyotard with his vision on the role of computers in society (see section 5.7);
* philosophers taking their starting point in religious beliefs; in the past we could find for example Friedrich Dessauer in that stream; nowadays there are people such as Schuurman (see section 5.8) who build their philosophy of technology on the conviction that behind the visual reality there are powers that we can not see, but that determine reality.

From this very brief survey, that is certainly a simplification and lacks nuance, we can see that the philosophy of technology reflects the whole spectrum of philosophical mainstreams as far as the theme of the relationship between humans and technology is concerned.

10. TEACHING AND LEARNING ABOUT TECHNOLOGY AS PART IF OUR BEING HUMANS

Teaching and learning about technology in the sense of technology being part of our being requires teaching strategies that are different from those that are needed to teach the aspects of technology that were dealt with in the previous chapters. To help learners acquire an understanding of this aspect, they need to be stimulated to reflect on this aspect themselves and to develop their own perspectives. Role-play and discussion groups can be appropriate strategies for that. In this chapter we have already come across movies as a way in which people have expressed their ideas about technology as part of our human existence. Such movies can be a stimulating vehicle to provoke discussions. In a similar way literature, painting and even music can be used. In general one can see that artists often have found ways to express their view on technology as part of our existence in a very though-provoking way, perhaps even more so than philosophers do with their books and papers. Still, those philosophical publications can help to interpret those movies, paintings, music and literature. There are books that specifically deal with one movie and show how it raises all sorts of philosophical discussions. For teachers such books are a valuable background resource when they want to use movies as didactical strategy for teaching about technology as part of our human existence.

Chapter 6

ETHICS AND AESTHETICS OF TECHNOLOGY

In the previous Chapter we have already seen that human values play an important part in technology. Some of these values have to do with what we consider to be good or bad things to be done. These are *moral values*. Ethics is the domain in philosophy that deals with moral values and issues. Other values are concerned with what we consider to be beautiful or ugly, with what we like or dislike. These are *aesthetical values*. In this Chapter we will discuss these two types of values in more detail. In section 6.1 we will discuss ethics and in section 6.5 a brief introduction to aesthetics in technology will be presented.

1. EXAMPLES OF MORAL ISSUES IN TECHNOLOGY

To get an impression of how moral issues are reflected on in ethics, we will take the following path: firstly, from a number of practical examples we will see that moral problems are a practical motive for seeking such reflections. Both engineers and non-engineers are faced with moral dilemmas and use such reflections to find appropriate ways of dealing with such dilemmas. Then we will see what the nature of a moral dilemma is. Here the role of logic in analyzing moral dilemmas will be discussed to show that ethical discussion are not just a matter of feelings and preferences but also include rational reasoning. Once we have seen what a moral problem is and how it can be analyzed, we are ready to explore different approaches to dealing with such dilemmas. As we will see there are at least three of such approaches. The final part of this section will be about two specific issues, namely the issues of risks and the aspect of collective responsibility. These two issues are not present in all moral dilemmas and that is why they will be dealt with only after we have discussed the more general issues.

Engineers as well as non-engineers are confronted with all sorts of moral issues. Let us firstly focus on the dilemmas with which engineers are confronted, as there is a growing amount of literature about that. Much of what is stated there can be applied in an analogous way to the ethical dilemmas that non-engineers are confronted with when using technology. In the 'engineering ethics' literature some examples have become true 'classics'. All of them deal with the issue of *safety*. One of these 'classics' is the explosion of the Challenger in 1986, which appeared to be the effect of the use of O-ring seals in the rocket. During test phases, engineers found that these rings malfunctioned under certain circumstances (in particular under low temperatures). These circumstances were not just hypothetic, but likely to occur during the launching of the rocket. Warnings were issued by the engineers, but the time schedule of these prestigious flights did not allow for drastic changes in the design. Thus the engineers were confronted with a dilemma: either to obey the interests of their company, or to obey the interests of the astronauts for whom a dangerous situation would emerge if the design would not be changed. A second example is the design of the Ford Pinto in the late 1960s. It was known from tests that in crash situations above certain speed the gas tank of this car could explode. But redesign of the car would mean loss of time and money for the company. Here again we see two clashing values: safety and economy. A third example of this type of moral dilemmas is the construction of the Bay Area Rapid Transit (BART) system in San Francisco. BART would have no operators and controllers because of the automatic train control system that was used. But during the construction engineers found out that there were serious safety risks. As the construction was already behind schedule, the project management ignored the engineers' concerns. It was only after a serious accident had happened that the engineers' warnings were taken into account.

So far for the issue of *safety*. A second field of moral dilemmas has to do with *environmental* issues. Often products can be produced cheaper at the cost of more damage to the natural environment. Designers are constantly confronted with dilemmas between financial and ecological constraints. The awareness of environmental damage due to technology emerged in the late 1960s. Since then the issue made a gradual shift from the political agenda towards the practice of engineers. A whole new field called 'green design' was developed in order to create tools and instruments to be used by engineers when practicing environmentally conscious designing. But such methods do not really dissolve the dilemmas between cost and environment.

Therefore in spite of the availability of the whole 'green design' toolbox, engineers have to make ethical decisions with respect to ecological matters.

A third field of moral dilemmas is related to information and communication technologies. Here engineers are faced with the problem of how to make information accessible while still preserving the *privacy* of the persons involved. Often these two requirements cannot be reconciled in the design and the engineers are then faced with a dilemma. Accessibility of information can be of interest for the police when searching for criminals, or for banks when deciding about funding of companies. But at the same time it is of importance to others that this information will remain confidential.

Then there is the whole field of designs for *military* use, which is also full of moral dilemmas. For some people the mere existence of this field already forms a moral dilemma: should one at all develop weapons of which the only possible use is to hurt or kill human beings. But even when this is accepted as morally acceptable, engineers can be confronted with all sorts of dilemmas that have to do with the extent to which the weapon may hit not only the target but also innocent people, with the sort of death that the weapon will cause (quick and painless or slow and painful). Here in fact the dilemma is between the value of one human (the one that is to be hit) and the other (the one that is to be protected or liberated by this action).

As we saw, engineers are confronted with ethical issues. This confirms what we have seen in the previous chapter: technology from the very beginning (the design phase) is not a neutral issue. That has not always been recognized by engineers, and still the education of engineers often lacks courses in which future engineers are taught skills to deal with ethical issues. Ethics was often seen as something that is only relevant for users. The engineer then would say: I just develop something that works according to the requirements, and whether this will result in blessing or curse is totally determined by the user. Now we know better. Also we have seen that ethics is more complicated that just telling what is good and what is wrong. Of course we know certain things we consider to be wrong. Bribery, espionage, sabotage are all practices we can find in engineering and that we generally consider to be wrong. But alas, ethics appears to involve more than just saying: do not bribe, spy or commit sabotage. Ethics involves dilemmas. And as we saw, there are at least four issues that can be the cause of moral dilemmas in technology: safety, environment, privacy and military. These dilemmas are problems to be solved by engineers. Engineers very well know that a good analysis of a problem is a necessary thing if we want to find proper solutions to problems. Therefore we will now turn to the analysis of moral problems and see how logic plays a part in that.

2.   ANALYZING MORAL DILEMMAS

For a decent analysis of what comprises a moral dilemma and what causes it, a survey needs to be made of who the involved parties are and what values they hold. Often the situation is more complex than just one party having one value and one other party having another value. In the case of the Challenger there were not only the company developing the O-ring seals and the astronauts, but also various agencies that produce and see to the application of legal requirements. Furthermore there is the government, for which the whole project is a matter of status and prestige. One of the parties involved of course are the engineers. They necessarily are, because if they have no influence on decisions, the whole concept of responsibility hardly makes any sense in their case. Responsibility assumes that one has possibilities to influence decisions. This is a very basic assumption in engineering ethics. In order to deal with this responsibility, engineers need to have competencies in *recognizing* and *analyzing* moral dilemmas, as well as capabilities in setting up proper *argumentations* for certain decisions. In this section we will discuss what it means to analyze moral dilemmas.

Apart from the parties involved, the dilemma itself needs to be analyzed. In some cases it can be the result of improper reasoning and finding that this is the case may open new ways of solving it. Here *logic* comes in. Logic is a domain in philosophy that deals with proper argumentation. Logical analysis can show whether or not certain reasoning is valid. Let us look more closely at the 'classic' example of the Challenger. The reasoning that was made by the engineers and that led to the dilemma was the following:

1. The O-rings do not function well when launching takes place at low temperatures;
2. During the launch of the Challenger temperature was low;
3. Failing O-rings will create a life-threatening situation for the astronauts;
4. Engineers in their work should not create designs that could be life-threatening to their users;
5. The replacement of the O-rings for something else will cause substantial delay in the project schedule;
6. It is in the interest of the company that there will be no delays in the project schedule;
7. Engineers should be loyal to their companies;

8. From (1), through (4) it can be concluded that the engineers should look for replacement of the O-rings;
9. From (5) through (7) it can be concluded that the engineers should not look for replacement of the O-rings.
10.Conclusions (8) and (9) are in conflict.

Statements (1) through (7) are the *premises* of the reasoning. They are as it were the input. The conclusions (8) through (10) are the output. And there are several processes that can lead from premises to conclusions, for example deduction and induction (later on we will deal with these processes, or *syllogisms*, in more detail). For proper reasoning at least two things are needed: all premises must be true, and the conclusion must be drawn in a proper way. This all seems to be the case, and the dilemma is not just a matter of improper reasoning. How then does the conflict between conclusions (8) and (9) emerge? Premises (1), (2), (3), (5) and (6) are not to be blamed for this. They are facts. The problem is that in this case we can not at the same time apply (4) and (7), which are moral norms. The engineers therefore will have to decide which norm should prevail. Deleting one of these two norms in the reasoning would make the conflict between (8) and (9) disappear.

As mentioned above, there are several ways of reaching conclusions from premises. Probably *deduction* is best known as a generally accepted mechanism for reasoning. There are two kinds of deductive syllogisms. The first runs as follows:

1. All men are mortal.
2. Socrates is a man.
3. From (1) and (2) it can be concluded that Socrates is mortal.

This is called the *modus ponens* syllogism.

A second deductive syllogism runs as follows:

1. All fish have gills
2. Whales do not have gills
3. From (1) and (2) it can be concluded that whales are not fish.

This is called the *modus tollens* syllogism.

Generally speaking, in deduction a general rule is used as one premise, a proposition about one particular case is another premise, and from those a conclusion can be drawn with respect to the particular case. In *induction*, again generally speaking, we reason the other way round: premises about particular cases lead to general rules as conclusions. These conclusions are not watertight. It may well be that other, not yet mentioned in the premises, cases may contradict the rule that was concluded. The conclusion is tentative. In some cases this is no reason for concern. But when induction is used to reach scientific theories many people think it is. Still today the philosophy of science wrestles with this problem of a lack of alternatives for induction. So far it seems we have to accept that scientific knowledge always has a tentative character. We cannot do much more than increasing the amount of support for the theory and with that the probability that the theory indeed is correct.

One particular improper way of reasoning that we can find in ethics is the *naturalistic fallacy*. This means that one concludes a norm from premises that only contain facts. What does that mean? Let us look at an example to understand what this fallacy is and why it is a fallacy indeed. A line of reasoning with respect to the environmental issue of using package could run as follows:

1. Plastic bags are made of plastic (this is a fact);
2. Plastic is not environmentally friendly (this is also a fact)
3. From (1) and (2) we conclude that we should not use plastic bags (this conclusion is a norm: it tells us what is good to do, or in this case rather what is not good to do).

Attractive as it seems at first sight (apart from the fact that premise (2) is not any more generally accepted), this is not proper reasoning, but an example of a naturalistic fallacy. Conclusion (3), which is a norm, does not follow from the facts (1) and (2) only. Someone who does not care very much about harm to environment, but rather looks for cheap and comfortable solution may totally agree with facts (1) and (2), but not with conclusion (3), which is a norm. In order to reach the conclusion (3) one more premise is needed:

2a.   We should not use materials that are not environmentally friendly.

This premise is not a fact, like (1) and (2), but a norm. And it is only by adding this norm to the premises that we have a valid conclusion. Anyone who accepts the norm that it is good to care for our environment and who also accepts that fact that plastic bags do harm the environment, will necessarily come to the conclusion that it is not good to use plastic bags. In the preceding example of the Challenger there was a correct reasoning because the conclusions were norms that were derived from a set of premises containing both facts and norms. Although the mistake to conclude norms from facts seems to be pretty obvious from this example, the naturalistic fallacy occurs many times in ethical reasoning, as we can all find when we read our newspapers carefully. Sometimes this fallacy is used by accident; sometimes it is consciously used to reach a conclusion that fits ones interests.

Now that we have seen the nature of moral problems it is time to see how different people use different approaches to solve moral problems.

3. DIFFERENT APPROACHES TO DEALING WITH MORAL ISSUES

Different people confronted with the same moral problem will make different decisions about that. Why is that? Maybe they do not agree on facts that support certain moral argumentations. We have seen an example of that: disagreement about whether or not plastic is harmful to the environment (or at least more harmful than other materials that could be used for bags) will probably lead to different conclusions about whether or not to use plastic bags. But there can also be disagreement about the norm premises of the argumentation. Is it really true that we have to avoid all use of environmentally unfriendly materials? Is such a general norm appropriate for moral reasoning in this case? Indeed there are alternative approaches. In general three different approaches can be distinguished. Each of those will be discussed now. And each of them can be found in technology.

3.1 An approach based on virtues

One approach to ethical issues is to take as a reference the moral qualities that someone, for instance an engineer, should have. In general such qualities can be honesty, compassion, respectfulness, etcetera. Each moral decision is judged against such qualities or *virtues*. The decision that seems to be most in line with the relevant moral virtues is regarded to be the best decision, even it is means that certain rules are broken or negative effects are the consequence. Based on the virtue of care for a fellow-human in need, one may decide to offer shelter to an innocent man that is hunted by mislead police officers. This breaks the rule that one should not act against the law. It may have negative impacts for the protector, as he may be taken captive as well when his protégée is found. But in the virtues approach all that does not weight against the virtues as a basis for moral decisions. One of the most famous philosophers that proposed this approach was Aristotle in his book on Nicomachean ethics. The highest virtue for Aristotle was to find the right middle between extremes. For example, in a good life one seeks a middle position between being avaricious and never spending money for pleasure, and being wasteful and spending lots and lots of money on luxury issues.

Do we find the virtue approach in technology? Yes, indeed. Textbooks on engineering ethics mention virtues such as: honesty, truthfulness and reliability. Such virtues can be found in ethical codes that professional engineering organizations have issued. In the 1990 IEEE (Institute of Electrical and Electronics Engineers) codes, for example, we find that engineers should be honest in stating claims or estimates based on available data (by the way, the first IEEE ethical codes date from 1912!). In general the engineer should have an awareness of responsibility. The decisions engineers make can have great impacts on other people's lives. Many cases of whistle blowing (a term commonly used for cases in which an individual engineer calls for attention to a certain bad practice in a company, even though this may create risks for his or her position in the company) emerge because an engineer experiences a conflict between his or her own feelings of responsibility towards the safety of the future user, or the environment, and the process in the company that is based on the companies interests (for example the financial interests or the reputation of the company). Evidently companies often have a ambiguous attitude towards a virtue-based ethical approach: on the one hand when asked they will emphasize that it is important that the individuals have virtues, but when it comes to practical decisions, it is often not appreciated when engineers let those virtues prevail over company rules. But in the world outside the company virtue-based behavior is better appreciated. It may well happen that governments will support whistle blowers and sometimes even prevent that they are disadvantaged because of their virtuous behavior.

3.2   An approach based on consequences

A second approach to moral problems takes *consequences* as a basis for moral decision-making. It requires an estimation of the totality of all effects on all actors involved to see what decision has the best overall consequence. Often 'best' is taken to be 'what produces most happiness'. If one decision makes one man happier and four people less happy, and an alternative decision makes four people happier and one man less happy, than the last decision is better than the first in this effect-oriented approach. This may be in spite of rules and virtues. "Stealing a chocolate bar in a shop makes me happier, and as probably the shop owner will not even notice the loss of only one of so many chocolate bars, it makes no person less happier, this act is morally permissive", one could argue in this approach. The overall consequence is positive, so the act is morally OK, even though rules are broken (by law it is not permitted to steal in shops) and virtues are neglected (being honest to the shop owner). Do we find this approach in technology? Again the answer is affirmative.

In Chapter 4 *technology assessment* was mentioned as a process to seek out the possible consequences of a technological decision. In technology assessment usually the following path is followed: (1) decisions are made on what technology will be the focus of the study, (2) a description of that technology, including its core technology and supporting or enabling technologies will be made, including the expected developments in that technology, (3) an analysis will be made of all social actors that are somehow involved in the process, either as technology developers, technology users, technology regulators, or other parties, as well as their interests and their possibilities to influence the development, (4) an analysis will be made of all effects that can be expected when a certain decision is made, usually in the shape of an impact tree, and if necessary several scenario's for such impact trees will be elaborated, and (5) then options for cutting and pruning the impact tree will be investigated: can undesired effects be avoided by cutting a branch in the tree or can desired but no yet expected impacts be created by pruning the tree. This way decisions are sought that give the most positive effects for the largest group of people. Although 'most positive' could be taken in an economic sense, this is certainly not the atmosphere from which the idea of technology assessment emerged. The idea behind technology assessment was to enable ethically sound decision making about technologies, with not only engineers involved, responsible as they may be, but with the whole community that is to be effected by the technological development. There is a more limited type of technology that focuses on the environmental effects of technological development. This type of assessment is called: environmental impact assessments. In some countries they are mandatory for companies that seek government permission to build a new plant or construct a new highway.

3.3   An approach based on rules

Thirdly, there is a moral approach in which rules are the core of the moral decision-making. Rules are to be obeyed, irrespective of the situation.

"Thou shalt not kill" holds both for soldier and for citizen. Based on this rule pacifists can argue for their decision not to serve in the army. Always tell the truth. This could be the motive for a doctor always to tell his patient what his or her disease if, even in cases where the patient psychically is not ready yet to hear such news. One of the better-known philosophers, who proposed such an approach, is Immanuel Kant. He distinguishes between two sorts of commands or *imperatives*: hypothetical and categorical. Hypothetical imperatives are of the following kind: if you want X, do A. You need not always do A, but only when you want X to occur. *Categorical imperatives*, to the contrary, always should be done, and Kant gives them a prominent place in his ethics. The categorical imperative that Kant is best known for runs as follows: Act in such a way that it is reasonable to accept that all people would act in the same way. According to this rule, stealing is morally problematic. It is not possible that someone would steal while wishing that everyone would act in that way. The result would be chaos, because everyone would steal from everyone (in fact this may result in me loosing again my stolen chocolate bar because someone else steals it from me). On the other hand, helping people in need would be a morally desirable act, because it would be great if all people would act in such a way. And again we ask the question: do we find this approach in technology? And again, the answer is: yes we do.

Many technological business corporations nowadays have ethical codes. These are general guidelines for ethical decision-making that the employers are supposed to follow when making decisions in which moral considerations play a part. But not only corporations issue such codes. Professional engineering associations also publish such codes and expect their members to act according to these guidelines. IEEE was already mentioned earlier. In their 1990 Code of Ethics we find, among others, the rule "to reject bribery in all its forms". In other words: bribery should always be refused, irrespective of the consequences, and irrespective of one's own personal values. On the Internet one can find numerous examples of such *professional ethical codes*. A quick survey of those will make clear that not all of those guidelines are of an *algorithmic* character; in other words, offer a clear sequence of actions that can only be interpreted in one unique way. Many of them are more of a *heuristic* nature. They do not contain exact rules, but rather suggestions about possible direction in which solutions might be found. But they do somehow give directions and therefore can be seen as examples of the rule-oriented moral reasoning approach in technology.

3.4 Solving ethical problems as if they were design problems

At first sight it may seem that solving a moral dilemma is a matter of choosing between two or more conflicting values. But Caroline Whitbeck has suggested a more creative approach, namely to treat a moral dilemma as if it were a design problem. Design problems and moral problems have in common that they are ill-defined. That makes them different than many of the problems scientists are faced with. Scientists are, for example, faced with problems to determine the relationship between two variables. Solving that problem may be difficult, but the problem itself is well defined. Both design and moral problems often are not well defined. Therefore Whitbeck advises to treat moral problems as if they were design problems. Design is not just a matter of choosing between alternatives. It can also be the creation of new alternatives. Such alternatives may help to avoid the dilemma that we find in moral problems. Let us go back one more time to the Challenger example. We have seen that choosing between one of the norms 'creating life-threatening situations to users is not good' and 'being loyal to the company is good' was a possible way out of the dilemma. But it is not the only one. In principle one could think of possibilities to make minimal changes in the design that do not cause much delay in the project schedule but do increase the safety of the O-rings under high temperature circumstances. The approach than is not to challenge the norm premises, but the fact premises. Whitbeck suggests that it would help to solve moral problems by looking at how designers solve design problems. In Chapter 4 we have seen that designers use various methods and tools to do their design work. Perhaps such methods and tools could also be developed and used for solving moral problems in technology.

4. TWO SPECIFIC ISSUES IN MORAL DILEMMAS

So far we have discussed issues that hold for all moral problems in technology. In this final section two particular issues will be dealt with that we do not find in all moral problems in technology, but only in specific cases.

4.1 Dealing with risks

Our discussion on the ethics of technology is not complete without paying attention to the issue of *risks*. The concept of risks has to do with chance and uncertainty about the future. A lot of debates about design decisions would be a lot easier if we would know exactly the effects of our design decisions. But we do not. That also holds for safety aspects. We never know whether our design will behave in a sufficiently safe way. But it would cost too much, if at all it were possible, to design the artifact in such a way that all risks would be excluded. We are almost forced to allow a certain risk. But how far can we go with that? Of course there is always the pressure to make the artifact as cheap as possible. But when is it no longer responsible to allow for more risk in order to get a cheaper design? The problem is that the mere concept of risk has not only to do with objective numbers, but also with feelings that people have about the seriousness of certain effects. Besides that we have to take into account both the chance that a certain accident will occur (assuming that it is possible to make good calculations for that), but also the seriousness of the effects. Maybe an explosion in a nuclear reactor is extremely unlikely to happen, but once it happens the results are disastrous, not only because of the number of people that may be affected, but also because of the way they are affected (involving perhaps many slow and painful deaths even in coming generations). But how must one balance the objective numbers (for instance the chance that an accident will happen) against the subjective feelings about the seriousness of an accident? This makes discussions about risks extremely difficult. Yet, engineers will have to engage in such discussions, and it is necessary for them to be aware of the choices they make in the approach to moral issues they use and that they make use of logic as a support for proper reasoning.

The issue of risk has led to the *precaution principle* that can be used as a guideline for decisions about technological developments in which risks are difficult to estimate. This principle tells engineers always to stay on the safe side. If there is substantial uncertainty about the possible damage that could be caused by a certain technological development, the precaution principle says: do not proceed. This principle is an example of a rule-based ethical approach.

4.2   Collective responsibility

Technology and engineering in general are not done by individuals but by groups. In the chapter on technological processes we have seen that design is often a matter of group work. This has implications for the ethics in technology and engineering. When a disaster takes place due to technological failures, the whole company or group who delivered the technology will be held responsible. Responsibility in technology does not only have an individual character, but also a *collective*. This makes things complicated when it comes to ethical considerations in technological developments. If responsibility is primarily a collective matter, how can individuals feel responsible? Each individual can defend him- or herself by pointing out that (s)he was only a small part of the whole enterprise and that it would not have been possible anyway to change the process on his or her own. Philosophically the issue here is whether there can be something like a 'group mind' that each of the individuals share and that will have the virtues of honesty, truthfulness and reliability that each of the individuals in the group should also have. This, of course, is a problematic concept and many philosophers reject it. In practice many companies try to create a certain group feeling. But it can be questioned if that is different from communality in feelings in each of the individuals. The group mind is some sort of mysterious separate entity, but just the communality in the individuals' feelings. The collective aspect is in the fact that being a member of the group creates a certain commitment towards that communality.

Due to the fact that technological developments increasingly involve different groups of people (engineers, managers, politicians, users), the issue of collective responsibility becomes more and more important. A consequence is that it becomes more and more difficult to find out who can be held responsible when a technological development leads to a disaster. Unfortunately this goes together with the fact that such complex developments are the most difficult to manage and therefore are more apt to flaws, and as such developments usually are so complex because they are also large-scale developments, the impact of these flaws can be very great. And if in such a situation there is no clarity about who can be held responsible for what, the chance of mistakes is large, because all people will be aware that even if they make a mistake it will be hard to identify them as the cause of the mistake.

Having explored the various aspects of moral values in technology, we now turn a second type of value: aesthetical values.

5. AESTHETICS IN TECHNOLOGY

About aesthetics we will be briefer. Not because it is less interesting, but because much less has been written about aesthetics in technology than there has been written about ethics in technology. In many technological domains, ethical issues are more prominent than aesthetical issues. Mechanical engineers designing a new type of engine do not bother much about aesthetical values. Most people do not even get to see it, so why make any effort to let it evoke aesthetical appreciation? Aesthetics is involved with how technological artifacts can evoke such positive feelings as the experience of beauty and happiness. Aesthetics in our time is also related to our personal identity and lifestyle. In general the importance of aesthetics in our culture has increased in the past decades. Thereby all our human senses can be involved: seeing, hearing, touching, smelling, and tasting. If we see movies in which festivals in the Baroque period are played, such as in the movie Vatel, we see that all the senses are addressed: there are colorful spectacles (seeing) with beautiful music (hearing), and a banquet with lovely food (tasting) that has been displayed in a beautiful way (again: seeing) and smells inviting (smelling). People are seated on chairs with soft and comfortable seats (touching). Everything has been done to please all the senses.

Although aesthetics can be relevant in various sorts of technological domains, there are two domains where it is of particular importance, namely architecture and industrial design. Both of these domains can almost be regarded as a sort of mixture of engineering and arts. Architects need to design constructions that are technically sound and get appreciation for their appearance at the same time. The same holds for industrial designers. Their mass-produced consumer goods should function well and look attractive at the same time. But when do we appraise an artifact for having 'beauty' or in general: aesthetical qualities? This is what aesthetics as a domain in philosophy is concerned with.

We will first focus on aesthetics in architecture. One of the ways to analyze the aesthetical values of a building is to seek for what symbols it uses to express certain values. Let us take the famous architect Antoni Gaudi as an example. His designs are mainly found in the city of Barcelona in Spain. Probably his most famous design is the Sagrada Familia cathedral. In this church we find numerous ways in which certain values have been expressed. In particular Gaudi's appreciation for the beauty of nature has resulted in all sorts of interesting details in his buildings. One of his statements was that nature always had many colors. For that reason he often used broken pieces of glazed ceramics to give brilliant color to curved surfaces. His motive for using curved surfaces and avoiding strait lines also is a principle that he had derived from nature. In nature one does not find strait lines, was his opinion, and this idea was reflected in his buildings. A comparison of the two façades of the Sagrada Familia that have been finished so far shows a great contract. The façade that depictures Christ's birth is full of details and makes a baroque impression. This illustrates the abundant joy that was preached by the angels to the shepherds. But the façade that depictures Christ's suffering and death on the opposite side of the church is totally different. It is very simple and modest and all the figures are depicted more symbolically than realistically. This fits well with the idea that Christ's death is something very sad; even though its purpose was good (it was Good Friday after all). The interior of the church is still largely incomplete, but already it can be seen that Gaudi has used tree-shaped columns in his masterpiece. Again here we find a reference to nature as the ultimate designer. In the church there is a small exhibition about all the analogies with nature that Gaudi has used in his buildings. The beauty of this impressive church is not in the least because of all these symbolical expressions of certain values that Gaudi has used in his designs.

In a similar way architects in earlier times have also used other ways of expressing values in their buildings. Gothic cathedrals, for example, reflect the idea that God is almighty, but at the same time close to humans. Here Gothic cathedrals contrast with roman cathedrals that are like fortresses and display Gods power more than his nearness. Gothic cathedrals on the one hand always point upwards with their enormous height, but at the same time give light every chance to come in and give an overwhelming feeling of light from heaven being near to us. They also display a vision on men as humble and small. Everyone who has entered a Gothic cathedral will recognize this feeling of being only a small being in this enormous space of the building. So the beauty of the building has to do with the way it expressed ideas about one's view of the world (or one's metaphysics as this is also called in philosophy), and one's view on man.

A second engineering field where aesthetical values are prominent is industrial design. As in architecture, here too we find a close relationship between technology and the arts. Industrial designers traditionally were primarily concerned with the outside appearance of a new product, usually a mass produced consumer product. Nowadays they scope often has broadened to functionality as well. In that case usually their position in the development process a shifted from being involved only in the final part of the process (when all technicalities had been decided on and only the cover had to be designed) to an involvement earlier on when decisions are made about functions that will be realized. Often they are called in when experiments with customers are to be conducted and mockups or prototypes are to be tested on consumers. But still today their main focus is the feelings of beauty and happiness that can be evoked by the product. What shapes, colors, smells, sounds and textures evoke such positive feelings is a matter that changed through times. Industrial designers have to keep track of such trends and try to translate them into concrete shapes, colors, smells, sounds and textures for their products. All human senses can be involved in this, and industrial designers will seek to exploit all possibilities.

The above is certainly not all there is to say about technology and aesthetical values. Technology more and more plays a role in enhancing the expression of aesthetical values in arts. One could, for example, think of the way computers are used by artists to create almost totally new forms of art ('computer art'). One could also think of the way new materials of production processes can provide new means for artists to add beauty to their works of art. And numerous other examples can be added to these two. A systematic discussion about such use of technology in art would take us into the field of philosophy of art. As this book is primarily on the philosophy of technology, the role of technology in art will not be discussed further here, exiting as it may be.

A final remark that should be made is that in aesthetics, like in ethics, logic can be used to enable discussions about beauty that exceed the level of mere emotions and individual experiences. Whether or not an object should be considered to be beautiful can be reasoned in the same way an activity can be analyzed to be moral or immoral. In general one can distinguish three types of reasonings. Theoretical reasonings result in conclusions that contain facts. Ethical reasonings result in conclusions that contain dispositions for action (what should be done, or what should not be done). Aesthetical reasonings lead to conclusions that contain appreciations of experiences (seeing this object we think it is beautiful or it is not). In aesthetical reasonings the same rules of logic hold as for other types of reasoning. So it is possible to discuss about taste.

6.   TEACHING ABOUT ETHICS AND AESTHETICS IN TECHNOLOGY

Perhaps the areas of ethics and aesthetics are the ones in which the human decision-making aspect of technology is most prominent. Here every suggestion that technology is just a matter of neutral research and development are immediately obvious to be invalid. Therefore these areas should have a proper place in the teaching about technology. They very clearly show the human character of technology. On the Internet one can find numerous examples of case studies that can be used to teach ethical analyses to pupils and students of various ages. For aesthetics alas there is not such an extensive set of examples available yet.

The teaching of these values requires different didactical strategies than for teaching, for instance, certain knowledge or skills. In fact here we can refer to the same kind of didactical strategies as in the previous chapter: role-play and discussion groups here too are obvious candidates. Only by experiencing what it is to develop values in one self, one can really understand what they are like. As in the previous Chapter, here too movies can be mentioned as a practical means for evoking discussions. Books have been written to make explicit what ethical issues can be found in specific movies (for example for the Star Trek series). Such books can be helpful for educators to recognize chances for starting ethical debates with such movies as an attractive and motivating trigger. In Chapter 9 the use of media will be discussed in more length.

Probably the fact that logic can be used in ethics and aesthetics is the most surprising element in teaching and learning about technology, and certainly this is not an obvious issue. It is important that learners get to realize that both in ethics and aesthetics. We can only have fruitful debates when we try to get above the level of mere emotions and individual experiences. Many discussions in ethics and aesthetics were fruitless because there were flaws in reasonings that no one noticed because no one made the effort to analyze those reasonings. Teaching and learning about ethics and aesthetics in technology can improve that. This can also take away the fear that some people have with respect to teach ethical and aesthetical aspects of technology, because they are afraid that it will result in indoctrination. This need not be the case. Teaching about ethical and aesthetical aspects of technology should be aimed at helping learners to develop their own opinions in a proper way by using proper reasoning, independent of what beliefs or convictions they may have as a reference.

Chapter 7

LEARNERS' PHILOSOPHIES ABOUT TECHNOLOGIES

In Chapters 2 through 6, a description of contemporary insights in the philosophy of technology has been presented. This is what philosophers say technology is. But how about non-philosophers? What perception of technology do they hold? For education we are particularly interested in pupils' and students' ideas about what technology is. It is also interesting, though, to compare their views on technology with those that we find among the general public. That is what this chapter is about.

1. PUPILS' AND STUDENTS' CONCEPTS OF TECHNOLOGY

There are two kinds of ideas that pupils and students can have with respect to technology: ideas about what it is (those we will call: concepts of technology), and ideas about how to value it (those we will call: attitudes towards technology). Later on (in section 7.2) we will see that those two kinds of ideas are related. Now let us first try to get an impression of both separately.

Pupils' and students' attitudes towards technology have been investigates in the past decades. Such studies have been conducted in both industrialized and developing countries. Although different research studies show different results on the level of details, there is much communality in the findings of those studies. Perhaps the most striking result is that pupils and students of the four views of conceptualizing technology (as artifacts, as knowledge, as processes, and as volition) most readily recognize the artifact dimension. If an average pupil or student is asked if (s)he can describe technology, the most probable answer is a list of technological artifacts. And most pupils and students have no problems in mentioning a whole variety of artifacts: radio, television, lasers, robots, and many others. But on second inspection, the list is not as rich as it may seem to be at first sight. The first limitation is the prominent place of the computer in the lists that pupils and students generate. Technology is in the very first place: computers. But this is not the only bias in the pupils' and students' concept of technology. A second bias is that technology is primarily 'high tech'. Once in an interview a 13-year-old boy responded to a researcher's question about what technology is by mentioning the steam engine. But he hasted to take back his answer by stating that this was not an appropriate example of technology, because it was too old. Clearly something has to be at least a 20th century invention in order to be called technology. The same result was found when a researcher gave a list of devices and activities, ranging from lasers and robots to wooden spoons and plastic cups to pupils and asked them to rank the items in order of 'being technological'. Quite convincingly, the laser and robot type of devices were ranked highly and the wooden spoons and plastic cups never made it to the top of the list (in most cases they ended up all the way down to the bottom). A factor analysis on the data revealed that pupils and students in their minds group the devices according to their level of sophistication ('high tech' versus 'low tech'), and the more sophisticated the devices, the more right they seem to have to be called technological. Perhaps surprisingly pupils in developing countries also tend to emphasize 'high tech' in their mental concept of technology. Perhaps this is a consequence of the fact that 'high tech' in such countries is often seen as an important factor in upgrading the level of development in that country. 'Technology' then is all these almost magic things that can help the country get to the level of modern, industrialized countries. In general we can see that children reflect what society tells them about technology. Watching television and reading magazines constantly enhances the idea that technology is 'high tech'. No wonder that their ideas of what technology is have become so narrow in the course of time.

The focus on artifacts by far outweighs the awareness of other dimensions in the concept of technology. Technology is hardly ever seen by pupils as something that has to do with knowledge. At best it has to do with applying knowledge from other fields, and science is the first candidate for delivering such knowledge. But even this is not very clear to pupils. Many of them either they state that science and technology are totally different and unrelated, or they say there is no different (thereby meaning that it is science that brings forth all the devices, and that technology is just another word for science). Only few recognize that science and technology are separate entities that mutually influence each other. Knowledge from other fields, such as knowledge about humans, knowledge about finances or laws, is almost never mentioned as a resource for technology.

The processes dimension too is only weakly represented in pupils' and students' concepts of technology. If at all activities are mentioned, it is the making and using processes most of the times. Only few pupils and students seem to realize that design in an important activity in technology. Apparently they conceptualize technology primarily with its outcome and not with its origin. Creativity, innovation, and fantasy are words than one will not find very often in young people's answers to the question what characterizes technology.

With respect to the human and social aspects of technology we can observe that young people often see technology as something positive. There are not that many pupils and students that show awareness of the negative impacts of technology. Maybe this is because of their strong focus on technology as artifacts. It is their direct experience that these artifacts often make life easier and more comfortable, and the negative impacts of technology are at a different level that they do not yet get to see or that does not yet appeal to them very much.

From this we can conclude that the image pupils and students have of technology is often narrow and biased. It reflects the way technology is presented to them in commercials and popular magazines. In those media technology is always the new high tech stuff that one should buy immediately and enjoy. It reveals the processes of designing and making that precede the availability of these gadgets. Without awareness of those processes it is also improbably that one realizes that technology is a matter of human decision making in which knowledge plays a part. As a result only the artifacts dimension of technology has a sound place in pupils' and students' concepts of technology, and the knowledge, processes, and human dimension remain hidden in the dark.

2. PUPILS AND STUDENTS' ATTITUDES TOWARDS TECHNOLOGY

Studies into pupils' and students' attitudes towards technology generally indicate that they have positive feelings about technology. Both boys and girls express an interest in technology. There are, though, significant differences between boys and girls in many studies. Boys often appear to have more interest than girls have. Although this sounds like a stereotype, alas it appears still to be reality. An interesting outcome in some of the studies is that the less positive attitude (in terms of interest) with girls is related to a narrower view they have of technology. In the previous section we have seen that pupils' and students have an artifact-oriented view of technology. This holds for girls even stronger than for boys. And also it appears that this focus on artifacts, rather than on the human and social aspects of technology, makes them less interested in technology. That fits well with many other studies into gender aspects of interests, from which we know that girls more than boys are interested in human and social issues. If technology in their view has to do more with artifacts than with humans, then their conclusion is that technology for them is of less interest than other subjects in which human and social aspects are more prominent. It is noteworthy that what is called 'interest' in these attitude studies, probably is strongly associated with curiosity and the excitement of the unknown. This can be concluded from the fact that in almost all studies into interest in school subject, the interest in these subjects decreases once the lessons have started. It is not very probable that all teachers in all school subjects would fail so seriously in maintaining the pupils' interest in that subject. It is more probable that interest decreases because the subject has lost some of its myth because now pupils know a bit about it.

There are more dimensions in the pupils' and students' attitudes than just interest. Pupils and students' also say that technology is important for their lives. We have already seen that they can mention a whole lot of examples of artifacts, and apparently they recognize that all these artifacts together make an important part of their daily lives. Furthermore they mostly express the opinion that technology has a positive role in their lives. There are relatively few pupils that can give balanced opinions in which both positive and negative effects of technology are taken into account. This should worry us. It means that many pupils lack the ability to make a critical assessment of technology. They are rather uncritical consumers. So if we see critical consumership as an important part of the technological literacy that we would like each citizen to have, there is still a lot of work to be done by those who teach about technology. Both girls and boys think that technology is something for both genders. This, though, in the case of girls is a rather theoretical point of view, because only few girls say that they themselves would indeed like to have a technological profession. They certainly think that there should be women in engineering, but not them. In that respect we have to be careful with our interpretation of their positive remarks about interest and relevance of technology.

3.   THE GENERAL PUBLIC'S PERCEPTION OF TECHNOLOGY

So much for young people. How about adults? Does wisdom come with age in this respect? To some extent: yes. But still, there is much to be desired.

Two major studies into the general public's attitude towards technology are the National Science Foundation (NSF) study in the USA and the Eurobarometer studies in Europe. The NSF study Science & Engineering Indicators 2002 showed that adults in the USA are moderately interested in science and technology. Many of them do not feel well informed about science and technology. They tend to seek their knowledge on television but find that prime time television does not pay much attention to science and technology. Those who really want to find out more do so by exploring via the Internet. In general the attitude towards science and technology is positive. Many technologies are expected to contribute positively to the quality of life: solar energy, computers, telecommunications, the Internet, and to a lesser extent space exploration. Clear exceptions in the positive feelings about science and technology are genetic engineering and nuclear power. It is striking that the general public still seems to have high expectations of basic research, even when it does not lead to industrial applications. In December 2001 the European Commission published the Eurobarometer on public understanding of science and technology in Europe. In this study too we find a majority of people stating that they feel poorly informed about science and technology and that television are their main source of information about science and technology. And here too, we find the positive attitude towards basic research. A large majority thinks that there should be social control of science and technology, and scientists and engineers certainly do not belong to the professions in which the general public has high confidence. Both the NSF study and the Eurobarometer make no effort to find out if people understand the difference between science and technology. In 2001 the International Association of Technology Education (ITEA) commissioned the Gallup Organization to conduct a nationwide poll to find out the general public's knowledge of and attitude towards technology specifically. It appeared that for two thirds of the respondents the word 'technology' is almost synonymous for 'computers'. The term 'design' was much more associated with blueprints and drawings that with a creative problem solving process. There was certainly a desire to have a better understanding of how things work among the general public and they also believe technology should have a proper place in the school curriculum. Some questions about examples of simple technologies revealed that much is to be improved in the general public's current knowledge of technology. Also it appeared that the general public can not tell how science and technology are different.

The overall impression is that adults, like young people, often have a narrow concept of technology (computers mainly) and a positive attitude towards it.

4.   INTUITIVE TECHNOLOGICAL CONCEPTS

So far we have focused on concepts of and attitudes towards technology in general. Now we will go down one level in detail. In technology various concepts are used to understand why things function as they do. Engineers use such concepts when designing new artifacts. Those concepts are taught in schools and colleges as parts of the education of future engineers, and some of them are also regarded to be necessary elements in the education of all citizens (for example the concept of systems, also because it is of wider relevance than for technology only). To what extent do pupils and students have an understanding of those concepts even before they have been taught those concepts in school? Perhaps surprisingly we do not know that much about this. For whatever reason research into pupils' and students' intuitive understanding of technological concepts has not been popular so far. In this section a kaleidoscope is presented of some of the few studies that are available in this respect.

For a limited number of concepts in technology empirical studies have been conducted to find out to what extent pupils master these concepts intuitively. For these studies a variety of instruments has been used. Some studies worked with a paper-and-pencil assignment and a questionnaire to let pupils write their experiences in solving that problem. Other studies used observations and written protocols of interviews with pupils. Although the concept of systems is often mentioned as a key concept in technology because it is found in a great number of technological disciplines, so far no effort has been made to find out the extent to which young and adult people have an intuitive knowledge of that important concept. In that respect, educational research in technology is still way behind similar research in science education. There pre-concepts have been studied for most of the essential scientific concepts and principles.

In the area of construction the concept of stability is an important concept. Gustafson, Rowell and Rose in 1995 started a study into the pre-concepts 242 pupils in grades 1 to 5 were asked to come up with ideas to increase the stability of a rather unstable structure of which a drawing was shown to them. They appeared to be able to mention an impressive variety of possible ideas, but many of them were irrelevant. These ideas were said to be based on previous experiences with such unstable structures. The overall impression is that children show a creative capacity to come up with ideas, but do not have much knowledge about the crucial concepts and therefore many of their ideas are not usable. Classroom instruction appeared to have a positive impact on the extent to which pupils can discern between relevant and irrelevant ideas, but surprisingly they do not identify those classroom activities as a source of their increased abilities. Probably this is due to the fact that the classroom activities did not create a confrontation between their original intuitive understanding of the situation and the proper concepts that were taught in the classroom situation.

Related to stability is the concept of counterweight. Twyford and Järvinen investigated Finnish 5th grade children's understanding of this concept. A nodding toy was selected as the context for this. Semi-structured interviews following a practical assignment were used as the research instrument. The assignment was part of classroom instruction on the subject. Therefore the study did not measure intuitive concepts but rather those that had been acquired through instruction. The authors were rather positive about the pupils' abilities to use the concept of counterweight in analyzing the problem situation. Alas they did not make an effort to explain how the classroom activity had contributed to that. Therefore it remains unclear why the students' ability to reason with concepts after instruction seems to be so much better than studies into intuitive concepts.

The use of materials is an aspect of technology that is important in a variety of technological domains. Some studies have been conducted to find out to what extent pupils can make the connection between the nature of a material and its use in products. Davis, Ginns and McRobbie did this for 92 elementary school children in grades 2, 4 and 6. They used interviews following confrontation with pictures of a variety of technological devices (bridges, bicycles, carry bags, etcetera). It appeared that especially at younger ages pupils most times were able to identity the material that was used in a certain product, but they had difficulties to recognize that material properties are independent of the artifact in which they are used. Probably the awareness of artifact-independent properties requires a higher level of abstraction than artifact-related properties. These findings are similar to a study in France by Chatoney-Ginestié, who asked 6-year-old children to describe properties of a variety of objects. Here too the name of the material was much easier for the children to mention than the material properties. Also the notion that a product is 'made of' a material seems to be problematic for young children. The relationship between raw material and a finished product is not well recognized.

A similar study on concepts like strength as a material property, and stability of a construction was done by Parkinson, not with children but with student teachers, using observations during the execution of a practical assignment by 40 student teachers working in pairs. It appeared that even for these students some relationships were difficult to understand. Students appeared to have difficulties in relating different types of material strength (bending strength, pulling strength) to forces in a construction. The students referred to previous experiences with structures as the origin of their intuitive conceptions.

The concepts that are taught in technology education somehow have their background in engineering. But in order to be useable in educational settings, knowledge of these concepts needs to go through a transformation process. In particular in France there is an interest is the transformation from the 'reference situation' (the world of the engineers) and the educational situation. Durey published an article about the way electronics concepts need such a transformation. Alas still there is a great lack of empirical studies that show how this transformation process should take place. Probably this transformation is even more dramatic when concepts from science are to be used in technology education.

The kaleidoscope of research studies into technological concepts as held by pupils and students is yet quite limited. There is still a great need for this sort of empirical studies. Yet what is available confirms the main conclusions that has already been drawn from studies in science, namely that pupils and students already hold intuitive concepts before we start teaching about technology and these intuitive concepts should be taken into account if ever we want to influence them. In the next chapters we will see how this can be done.

5.   REFERENCES

In this chapter a number of references were mentioned that are not in the annotated bibliography (Chapter 11) because they are much more specific than the general literature that is listed in that bibliography. Therefore these references are listed below and not in Chapter 11.

Chatoney-Ginestié, M. (2003), Construction du concept de matériau dans l' enseignement des 'sciences et technologie' a l'école primaire: perspectives curriculaires et didactiques (unpublished Ph.D. dissertation). Aix-Marseille: Université de Provence.

Davis, R.S., Ginns, I.S. and McRobbie, C.J. (2002), 'Elementary school students' understandings of technology concepts', Journal of Technology Education, Vol. 14, No. 1, 35-49.

Durey, A. (1997), 'Transforming engineering concepts for technical and vocational teacher education in France', in: Vries, M.J. de and Tamir, A. (eds.), Shaping Concepts of Technology. From Philosophical Perspectives to Mental Images. Dordrecht: Kluwer Academic Publishers, 181-201. Reprint from International Journal of Technology and Design Education, Vol. 7, No. 1/2.

Gustafson, B.J., Rowell, P.M. and Rose, D. (1999), 'Elementary children's conceptions of structural stability: a three year study', Journal of Technology Education, Vol. 11, No. 1, 27-44.

Parkinson, E. (2001), 'Teacher knowledge and understanding of design and technology for children in the 3-11 age group: a study focusing on aspects of structures', Journal of Technology Education, Vol. 13, No. 1, 44-58.

Thomson, C. (1997), 'Concept mapping as an aid to learning and teaching', in: Vries, M.J. de and Tamir, A. (eds.), Shaping Concepts of Technology. From Philosophical Perspectives to Mental Images. Dordrecht: Kluwer Academic Publishers, 97-110. Reprint from International Journal of Technology and Design Education, Vol. 7, No. 1/2.

Twyford, J. and Järvinen, E.-M. (2000), 'The formation of children's technological concepts: a study of what it means to do technology from a child's perspective', Journal of Technology Education, Vol. 12, No. 1, 32-48.

Chapter 8

RECONCEPTUALIZING TECHNOLOGY THROUGH EDUCATION

We have seen what philosophers see as characteristics of technology in Chapters 2 through 6, and the extent to which young people and adults recognize these characteristics in Chapter 7. We can now ask the question: how can we change people's mental concepts of technology for the better? How can we create educational contexts that enable learners to get a better perspective on technology? In this Chapter some examples of that will be discussed. We will take the following route. Firstly, we will examine the content of curriculum documents in some countries where technology education already has a certain tradition, or where in recent years a lot of attention has been devoted to developing a new curriculum for technology education. We do that in order to see to what extent the content of these curricula stimulates development of balanced perceptions of technology in the pupils' and students' minds. Then we will discuss two strategies for improving those perceptions in educational settings. The first one is the use of case studies (whereby we will discuss both historical and contemporary case studies). This strategy was chosen because it is also used in philosophy of technology (in what is called the 'empirical turn', see Chapter 1). If philosophers nowadays use that strategy to clarify concepts of technology, then we can expect it also be useful for teaching those concepts. The second strategy is concept mapping. This strategy was chosen to be discussed because it is directly related to concept development.

1.   THE CONTENT OF CURRICULA

The first thing we can do to see if our education can help people to improve their view on technology is to examine the content of curricula. Is it possible that a curriculum is biased in such a way that it enhances misunderstandings in the learners mind rather than to get a better balance? That is the case, for example, when the curriculum only pays attention to the making process and always assumes that the design exists already. Learners in such a curriculum never get to see the creative process of solving design problems and therefore will not learn to recognize the importance of the design process in technology. Alternatively, a curriculum can be entirely focused on the process of designing without making explicit that knowledge of engineering concepts is a necessary condition for solving design problems properly. In such a curriculum the learners will get the impression that technology is equal to any kind of designing process, and the notion that a particular body of knowledge is related to the discipline gets lost. In cases where the curriculum clearly does not reflect the main characteristics that we have seen in the earlier chapters of this book, namely artifacts, knowledge, processes and volition, a first strategy toward proper reconceptualizing technology in the learners' minds is to adapt the content of the curriculum.

To what extent do existing standards and curricula take into account the philosophical insights that have been described in this book? To get an impression of that, we will examine some standards and curricula that have been made available widely. There is a difficulty in this because standards and curricula have a temporary character. In principle it is possible that examples that are used here may not even be part of educational practice when this book is published. For that reason a small selection has been made of standards and curricula that have been the outcome of major national projects and therefore can be expected to have a longer lifetime than standards and curricula that have been produced at a local level.

In the project "Technology for All Americans" standards for technological literacy have been described for teaching about technology in American schools for pupils in the primary and secondary level age. The term 'technological literacy' was used to indicate that teaching about technology does not only take place in dedicated school subject about technology, but also in other subjects and also in settings other than formal education. Also for those who are involved in teaching about technology in higher educational levels it is of interest to examine the "Technology for All Americans" standards as they also should be seen as a basis for further education. The references that are mentioned at the end of the report show many titles for the field of philosophy of technology. Evidently, a serious effort was made to build upon insights from the philosophy of technology in order to get a proper view on what should be taught and learnt to acquire technological literacy. The effort was successful in that all four ways of conceptualizing technology as they have been defined by Mitcham, and used in this book (technology as artifacts, as knowledge, as processes, and a volition) are clearly represented in the standards. There are twenty standards in the report, the first of which has an introductory character and deals with overall characteristics of technology. The remaining two standards in the first section, called The Nature of Technology, reflect the technology as knowledge idea. Here the core concepts of technology are listed as the content of the knowledge base of technology. The next four standards deal with the theme of Technology and Society and here we find the 'volition' idea elaborated. In the Design and Abilities for a Technological World sections, both comprising three standards, focus on the processes idea. In the final section, The Designed World, we find the artifacts idea, worked out in the areas of medical technologies, agricultural technologies, energy and power technologies, information and communication technologies, transportation technologies, manufacturing technologies, and construction technologies. In this respect, the standards of the Technology for All Americans project offer a good representation of the various ways of conceptualizing technology. This is not surprising because in the list of references we find several titles in the field of philosophy of technology. It is clear that the project has made a serious effort to take into account the philosophical insights in that literature.

The term "technological literacy" also features in a project that was conducted by the National Association of Engineers in the USA. This prestigious professional organization has shown considerable commitment to stimulating proper teaching about technology at all educational levels. A committee was set up to study the way technological literacy can be defined and promoted through education. The project resulted in a report "Technically Speaking". As in the standards project described earlier, this report too makes extensive use of philosophy of technology literature. Based on such literature, the report explicitly describes what it sees as misconceptions of technology, namely technology as merely applied science, and technological determinism.

As England and Wales probably have the longest tradition in technology education at the primary and secondary level, it is worthwhile to take a look at their national curriculum also. Since the introduction of the National Curriculum the content of the subject 'Design & Technology' has changed a number of times. But throughout the consecutive versions of the subject description, some overall characteristics seem to have remained constant. Currently the curriculum is described in terms of Attainment Targets that indicate what pupils should be able to do in the end, and Programmes of Study that indicate via what activities this should be accomplished. In general, the England and Wales curriculum has a certain bias toward design as part of the processes aspect of technology. The main focus of the curriculum was and still is on the process of designing. But this does not mean that the other aspects, namely artifacts, knowledge and volition, are all absent. Knowledge is explicitly mentioned as a separate category in the Programmes of Study for the various levels. In particular knowledge of materials and components is listed. Also the concepts of systems and control are part of the knowledge base of Design & Technology. Less prominent are the artifact and volition aspects. At some places in the description of Attainment Targets and Programmes of Study reference is made to the functioning of artifacts that should be understood by pupils. But this is done in a very shallow way of dealing with artifacts, and a basic insight such as the difference between proper and accidental use is not mentioned. Even more striking is the almost complete absence of the wider impact of technology on society. It seems that the whole curriculum is based on the role of pupils as designers, and not as users of new products.

Now for Australia. Here the situation is complicated by the fact that each state has its own curriculum, and there is not yet, such as in the USA with its Technology for All Americans project, a common framework for teaching about technology in primary and secondary schools. There was, though, a document that influenced developments in several states, published by the Australian Education Council in 1994. Emphasis was put on the process dimension of technology (no doubt this was inspired by the example in England and Wales). The text on Technology as one of the learning areas that were proposed stated that pupils should be "prepared for living and working in an increasingly technological world and equipped for innovative and productive activity". Although each of the States and Territories was autonomous in developing its own curriculum, the nationally produced document was used as a model by several of them. A first example is the state of Queensland. The curriculum in this part of Australia is structured as follows: there are four main domains namely Technology Practice, Information, Materials, and Systems. It is curious that Energy has not been identified as a separate domain, even though the systems approach that has been used strongly suggests that. The Technology Practice domain corresponds directly with the processes aspect that we met in the philosophy of technology. The main processes identified are: investigation, ideation, production and evaluation. The Information domain is not very specific for teaching technology. In this domain we find elements of the volition aspect in the philosophy of technology in that it focuses on users' needs and information ownership and control. The Materials domain is the only domain where the knowledge aspect is made explicit (of course the other domains assume the existence of that aspect also, but do not make explicit that it is a characteristic of technology). The Systems domain is the one where we find the artifacts aspect most clearly. Pupils are to get to know various familiar systems and how they function. Thus we see that all four aspects that we found in the philosophy of technology to some extent are represented in the Queensland curriculum. The second example to be investigated is the New South Wales curriculum for technology teaching. The name of the course is 'Design and Technology', which is a clear reference to the England and Wales situation, but for some grades the name is changed into Technology. Here the content of the curriculum is described in terms of three strands: knowledge, skills and attitudes. At first sight one could guess that these represent the knowledge, processes and volition aspects in the philosophy of technology and from that conclude that the artifacts aspect is missing. But the situation is more complicated than that. The Knowledge strand starts with a focus on the way technology influences society, and this reminds us of the volition rather than the knowledge aspect in the philosophy of technology. The second part of the Knowledge strand deals with knowledge of processes, and thereby refers to knowing-that much more strongly than to knowing-how (in Gilbert Ryle's terms; see Chapter 3). The knowing-how part is in the Skills strand. The Attitudes strand indeed deals mainly with the volition aspects of technology. Our conclusion here must be that the artifacts aspect indeed seems to get little attention. There are no outcomes formulated that deal with the nature of artifacts.

It must, of course, be emphasized that the analysis of curricula does not give any information about the quality of educational practice. The England and Wales curriculum may seem to have certain biases, but certainly there is excellent practice, based on many years of experience, in these parts of the UK. And it is beyond any doubt that the Standards for Technological Literacy in the USA certainly are not yet representative of what happens in the majority of schools. Yet, it is interesting to see how different countries have chosen different orientations in teaching about technology at the primary and secondary level. Our survey, limited as it is, also reveals that in some cases a careful study of the philosophy of technology could lead to a richer and more balanced curriculum. In Chapter 1 this was identified as one of the possible motives for taking notice of developments in the philosophy of technology. It appears now that indeed for teaching about technology it is

useful to see how technology nowadays is conceptualized in the philosophy
of technology, in order to provide a good image of what technology is.

2.   THE USE OF HISTORICAL CASE STUDIES

Historical case studies can be a rich resource from which educators can
draw to make clear to learners what the various characteristics of technology
are. This, of course, depends on the quality of the cases study descriptions
that are available, but fortunately historians of technology in the past
decades have done a lot of work to develop such case study descriptions. In
Chapter 3 we have already seen how the historical case studies on designing
aircrafts have enabled Walther Vincenti to come up with an interesting effort
to describe types of engineering knowledge. Let us here examine another
example of how historical information can be used to reshape learners'
concept of technology. The example is a case study in the history of
industrial research, namely the history of the Philips Natuurkundig
Laboratorium (this is its Dutch name; the English translation is Philips
Physics Laboratory). The history of an industrial research laboratory is a
quite suitable source to learn about the relationships between science and
technology. Industrial research laboratories are institutes where new
scientific knowledge is developed to create opportunities for technological
innovations and inventions. In such a laboratory there is a constant concern
about establishing fruitful relationships between science and technology, and
also there are tensions accompanying that concern. On the one hand people
working there see themselves as scientists for whom gaining knowledge is
almost an end in itself and publishing in academic journals is the most
important result of their work. On the other hand there is always awareness
that their work should provide a knowledge basis for the company to enable
the creation of new products, and in that light acquiring patents is a more
important outcome than publishing in journals. Also there are tensions in the
extent to which scientists claim freedom of choosing research topics. On the
one hand the industrial researchers want to be free to explore new fields for
which no application is yet foreseen but which are interesting from a
scientific point of view; on the other hand there are fields that product
divisions in the company see as strategically important and that they would
like to see being studied by the research lab. Examining the history of such a
laboratory can reveal different patterns of interaction between science
activities and technology activities and thus help us reconceptualize our view
on the science-technology relationship. Reconceptualizing is a proper term
here because most people already have an intuitive image of an industrial
research laboratory. Usually in this image an industrial research laboratory is

a place where scientists have almost complete freedom to study whatever they are interested in and that results in brilliant new ideas that have a great impact on the long term strategy of the company because of the extremely innovative products that result from the fundamental knowledge that the scientists come up with. This concept of an industrial research laboratory is associated with the idea that technology is the application of science. A historical case study like that about the Philips Research Laboratory can help us to become aware that such a naïve idea is only a partial truth and that there is much more to say about the science-technology relationship.

A description of 80 years of research at the Philips Natuurkundig Laboratorium (1914-1994) shows us that three different periods can be identified on the basis of differences in the science-technology relationship that was realized in the lab:

- in the first 30 years of the lab's existence, it was very closely tied to all other parts of the company. There was direct contact with the company's directors (in the early years the Philips brother Anton and Gerard) and when the directors decided that time was ripe to enter a new market, the laboratory went to work to realize this ambition by developing new knowledge and new products. It could also happen that the scientists had found something interesting that might result in a new product and then direct contact between the lab and the company directors would lead to a decision about this. Also there was good co-operation with the factories where the new products were to be made. In this period we see the development of scientific knowledge functioning in close relationship with the development of new technologies;
- in the second period, roughly speaking the next 25 years, the lab changed its strategy dramatically and became a place where basic research was seen as a high priority and the day-to-day concerns of product development and production were seen as improper tasks (such tasks should be done by other labs in the company, that were part of the various product divisions). The idea was that new fundamental knowledge would lead to revolutionary new products, to be further developed and detailed by the product divisions. To some extent this worked, but it also resulted in a rather frustrating relationship between the research lab and the product divisions because both parties felt a lack of commitment at the side of the other party. This is the period in which the 'technology as applied science' idea was practiced;
- in the next 25 years the economic decline forced the company to reconsider the role of the laboratory and made it redefine its strategy to become more directly focused on the needs of the product divisions. This was not a return to the first period. Not the company directors, but

individual, fairly autonomous product divisions decided about the company's product portfolio and the lab had to bargain with these divisions about their budget by offering contracts to them for research work. The division would then commission the lab to deliver specific knowledge that was needed for the development of a new product or of a particular part of a new product. In this period science was a servant to technology.

So what we see here is that there are at least three different patterns of interaction between science and technology and in that way the historical case study of the Philips Natuurkundig Laboratorium has helped us to refine our mental concept of an industrial research laboratory and of the relationship between science and technology.

3.   THE USE OF CONTEMPORARY CASE STUDIES

Not only historical, but also contemporary case studies can be used to give learners a better understanding of technology. Fortunately here too more and more of such case studies become available. Constantly new monographs are published that describe recent developments in technology, not only from a purely technical point of view, but also illustrating the full complexity of such developments due to the variety of scientific, technological and social influences. Here I would like to take one such a monograph as an example to illustrate this, namely the development of Glare, a new material that is now used for parts of aircraft, such as the impressive double-decker Airbus A380, in particular on the wings of the aircraft. Glare is the usual abbreviation of GLAss REinforced Laminates, a material that is light – which, of course, is important for an aircraft – and at the same time can substantially reduce crack growth in aircraft parts compared to crack growth in metal parts. Ad Vlot, who was one of the key players in the development of this material, wrote a book (published by Kluwer Academic Publishers in 2001 under the title 'Glare') about this material, from which we can draw a lot of useful information to be used in teaching about technology.

Vlot's book describes how the development of Glare with its undeniably positive material properties, and all sorts of factors that hampered acceptation of the material by aircraft companies. Because of the large risks that come with aircraft use, designers of new aircraft are rather conservative and not willing to embark in adventures with unknown outcomes. Glare as a composite material was a rather revolutionary change compared to the more traditional metallic materials (in particular aluminum). In spite of the fact that these metals had been found to have serious problems because of fatigue (the strength of the material decreases in time) and corrosion, an alternative as dramatically different as a composite material was not easily accepted. Another complicating factor was the different interests that were held by the various partners in the development: the Delft University of Technology, where knowledge development was important, the aircraft companies in different countries (Fokker in the Netherlands and Airbus as a European consortium), organizations that are responsible for independent inspection of the safety of aircraft, and so on. The European dimension even caused totally unforeseen problems such as the fact that the English term Glare in French sounds like 'glaire', which means slime, and which did not really sound as a positive recommendation for the use of this material on aircraft constructions. Of course there were many economic factors such as the price of the material and of applying it to parts of an aircraft. An ethical factor was the fact that in principle Glare was an environmentally friendly material compared to its current alternatives. Due to the low weight of Glare, the use of fuel by the aircraft would decrease, which would mean less use of natural resources and less emissions. The complex interactions between all these factors resulted in a struggle to get the material accepted for first appliance, which would last for several decades until finally Airbus decided to use Glare for certain parts in the new A380 (Vlot's story on Glare covers the period 1988-2001). Perhaps the fact that this was a revolutionary design anyway caused the designers to be less hesitant in accepting new materials for aircraft constructions. Vlot's description also reveals the interaction between the design work leading and scientific experimentation leading to new knowledge. In that respect the Glare story is a nice contemporary equivalent of the historical account of the Philips Natuurkundig Laboratorium that was discussed in the previous section of this chapter. Here too, we find different interaction patterns that confirm that 'technology as applied science' can not be accepted as a proper account of the relationship between science and technology. For Glare this has to do with the fact that, unlike for metals such as aluminum, in the case of composites scientific modeling does not easily lead to precise predictions of the behavior of the material. Apart from social factors, this was a technical barrier for the acceptance of Glare by the aircraft industries. Another analogy with the Philips Natuurkundig Laboratorium is the lab's scientists' strong belief in the inventions that keeps driving the development in spite of all resistance from outside.

4.   CONCEPT MAPPING AS AN EDUCATIONAL TOOL

While teaching about technology it would be nice to keep track of how education affects the learners' concepts. For that purpose the use of concept mapping can be a useful tool. Concept mapping is a way of externalizing the structure of concepts as they are in the learners' minds. Concept maps are drawings in which concepts are visualized as texts in balloons that are interconnected. Two balloons are connected if they represent concepts between which people see a relationship. An example of that is the following (derived from an article by Carole Thomson in the book 'Shaping Concepts of Technology', edited by De Vries and Tamir; see Chapter 11). To get an impression of primary children's overall concept of technology, a map was drawn of various topics that are involved in such a concept. Top of the map is the term 'technology'. From that term emanate the terms 'people', 'everyday things' and 'meeting needs'. Those are things technology is about. From the term 'everyday things' a next issue emerges by way of an example: 'mechanical things'. Then follow 'computers', 'modern resources', 'non-living systems' and artifacts'. From the term 'people' are derived further terms such as 'challenges', 'ideas', and from the latter: 'change', 'advancement' and 'new/modern'. The 'meeting needs' term leads to further terms as follows: 'human endeavor', 'application of science', 'working with others', and 'interacting with the environment'. All the time a next term emerges by way of associative thinking: what next term does each term remind you of? This process in the end led to a map consisting of no less than 42 terms. The map had both linear and circular parts. It appeared that children in two different schools had developed different overall concepts of technology. This was found by investigating the extent to which children made the various associations between terms in the concept map. In one school children appeared to focus on process terms such as 'use of resources', 'designing', 'making', 'investigating', and learning, while in a second school children more frequently mentioned the artifact aspects of technology, expressed in terms like 'mechanical things', 'computers', hydraulics', and 'electronics'. These children, contrary to the children in the first school, were aware of 'application of science' as a concept in the concept map. Thus the use of concept mapping revealed interesting differences between pupils in two schools, and these findings no doubt can be related somehow to the way teaching about technology was practiced in the two schools.

It is important to note that concept mapping should not be seen as a tool that can be used in isolation. Concept mapping needs to be embedded in broader educational strategies, in particular in cognitive apprenticeship. As describing that in more detail would lead us away from the specific interest in developing concepts that leads the selection of content for this chapter, and given the fact that there is ample literature on this strategy now, I will not discuss it any further here. For practical application, though, it is important to take notice of this broader strategic context for concept mapping.

Finally it is necessary to remark that concept mapping is a practical tool that helps to visualize how concepts are arranged in the pupils' minds, but not to develop a structure for concepts. In that sense we can only have limited expectations of concept mapping. Also we should realize that the use of concept mapping depends of course on the extent to which abstract concepts can form in the pupils' minds and this depends on age level.

Chapter 9

PRACTICAL ISSUES IN TEACHING ABOUT TECHNOLOGY

In this chapter some practical issues related to teaching about technology will be dealt with. Not all practical issues though, but only those that have to do with teaching about technology aimed at helping learners to acquire a proper concept of technology. After all, that is why we made our survey through the philosophy of technology: to find out what a proper concept of technology is. And as we saw, there is certainly good reason to make a very conscious effort to conceptualize technology in a proper way, because young people as well as adults can have all sorts of misconceptions. Besides that, existing curricula appear not always to capture the main aspects of technology. Even is they do, there are still all sorts of practical issues that need to be taken into account when teaching for a proper conceptualization of technology. Such issues will be discussed in this chapter.

1. DIFFERENCES BETWEEN DIFFERENT LEVELS OF EDUCATION

Building up a full and balanced concept of technology in the learners' minds is something that will happen in the course of the various levels of education that they go through. In that respect the ideal is a *continuous learning line*. At the moment this is often not yet the case. There are still countries in which *tertiary education* is the first opportunity for learners to become acquainted with what technology really is like. But that level of education is fairly specialized and providing an overall concept of technology is seldom seen as an educational task for that level. There are changes, though, in recent practice. In several countries the scope of *engineering education* is widened. This is a result of the fact that educators in engineering colleges and faculties increasingly become aware of the need to help their students get a clearer view of the social and ethical aspects of technology, in addition to all the highly specialized knowledge and skills that are taught. This awareness to some extent is the result of contacts with industries, where the same development took place. Product development in industry nowadays is a matter of careful listening to what markets and customers require. This forces industries to ensure that they have a workforce that is able to capture and understand those requirements and that is also able to transform them into product qualities. It is unthinkable that workers with a narrow, nuts-and-bolts oriented concept of technology would be able to do that. The result of all this is, that engineering programs increasingly incorporate courses on social and ethical issues in technology into their curricula. Students are trained in making analyses of moral dilemmas in engineering practice, they have to make modest technology assessment studies in order to get a feeling for the impacts of technology on society, they are taught to take into consideration environmental issues when doing engineering project work, and so on. For academic engineering programs this is often seen as a necessary component of an engineer's training at the academic level. Even more than vocationally trained engineers, the academically educated engineer should be knowledgeable about the nature of engineering and able to reflect systematically on the practice of engineering.

Although the development sketched above is already quite a progress compared to a situation in which engineers are educated in the traditional, much narrower way, it is not enough. If conceptualizing of technology does not commence until the tertiary level, intuitive concepts and attitudes with respect to technology may already have become fixed to such an extent that it is very difficult to modify them at that late stage. Therefore it is necessary that lower levels of education also include proper conceptualization of technology in the learners' minds. Probably the most important level for this conceptualization is the *secondary level*. Here too, positive developments take place. In an increasing number of countries governments have decided to have education about technology as a compulsory component of the education of all future citizens. Sometimes this is done in the form of a separate school subject or learning area, sometimes it is done by having a recognizable component on technology in a more comprehensive subject, or in an existing subject such as science education. In secondary technology education two sublevels can be distinguished: the lower level in which the overall characteristics of all technologies can be at the core of conceptualizing technology, and the higher level in which the particularities of different types of technologies can be explored. This last-mentioned level can then be a good preparation for tertiary education, because that level is specialized and a basic understanding of the differences between different technologies can help students to make a choice between the various areas of technological specialization. Psychology has shown that pupils must have reached a certain level of abilities to think in more abstract ways in order to be able to learn abstract concepts. In secondary education most pupils in theory should have reached that mental level. That means that teaching and learning the overall concept of technology and of specific concepts in technology should be feasible in secondary schools.

One level down, we have *primary education*. Here the main task in the continuous learning line can be to provide a first *orientation* on technology. This is a valuable preparation for teaching and learning technological concepts at secondary level. Primary education is probably the best phase for such an orientation for two reasons. In the first place, pupils at this age level are still quite easy in asking questions about what they experience. And asking questions about reality is the best entrance to getting to know the character of reality. Children can ask all sorts of questions starting with 'why', 'what' or 'how'. One could almost say that children still show a good philosophical attitude in that they are nor afraid of asking questions about the obvious. At higher age levels, pupils become more afraid of being laughed at when they ask such questions. A second reason why orientation on technology can have its best start in primary education is that there is no separation in subject areas being taught by specialized teachers. Here the one and only teacher teaching a class can freely move from one subject area to another. Thus a coherent and integrated view on technology can be developed.

But all this can only be realized by teachers who have been educated in such a way that they themselves have a proper concept of technology. This brings us back to the tertiary level, but now in the domain of *teacher education programs*. In such programs the development of a more sophisticated concept of technology should be an important aim, in addition to all other knowledge and skills that student teachers need to acquire. Strategies for setting up educational settings in which pupils and students can acquire a good concept of technology should be part of what is often called 'pedagogical content knowledge' (abbreviated as PCK). PCK in fact is the bridge between the content knowledge of the subject area (in this case: technology) and general theories about teaching and learning. In other languages it is indicated as Didaktik (German), didactique (French), didaktiek (Dutch), or other equivalents. This is sometimes confusing in international debates, as the term 'didactics' in English has a much narrower meaning and mainly refers to fixed teaching methods rather than to wider reflections on how teaching and learning takes place. It is important to notice that the terms like Didaktik, didactique and so on not only include the cognitive aspects of learning, but also the psychomotor and affective aspects.

Thus a learning chain of orientation, conceptualization, differentiation and specialization could provide a continuous learning line leading to a full and proper conceptualization of technology, in accordance with the ideas in contemporary philosophy of technology.

So far I have pointed out the importance of this learning line for the education of engineers. It is, however, of no less importance for the education of all other citizens. A good perspective on the true nature of technology is necessary to function in our contemporary technological world. This holds for the professional part of our lives as well as for the leisure part. Technology has pervaded all types of professions as well as most of the non-professional activities in our lives. For that reason not only future engineers need to go through a learning line as sketched above, but also future non-engineers.

2.   THE USE OF MEDIA

The use of modern media for teaching is often called *educational technology*. In itself this term covers well what it intends to say. But at the same time it causes confusion. Many people do not realize that educational technology and technology education are two entirely different things. Educational technology is the use of technology as a means for teaching about whatever (possibly technology, but not necessarily). Technology education is the teaching about technology (possible with the use of supportive technologies, but not necessarily so). The book 'Teaching About Technology' is on technology education; this particular section of the book is on educational technology.

There are several reasons for using new media in one's teaching about technology. In the first place there is a motivational reason for that. Many teachers have the experience that the use of new media excites pupils and students. They are more motivated to go through the content of a course when this course is supported by new media in which video fragments, animations, interactive information is offered to them. Research has confirmed the positive attitude of pupils towards learning about and with computers. A caveat here is that this effect probably is only temporary. After a while the new media are no longer experienced as 'new' and the excitement fades away. When the new media have been used to hide away a lack of relevance and interest of content, then this fading away will reveal shamelessly how poor the content actually was. The success of teaching about technology therefore should primarily be in its relevant and interesting content, and not in the way it was presented, although the presentation of course should also be well taken care of. In the second place the use of new media is almost unavoidable when the teaching about technology is to offer a valid representation of what goes on in professional practice. In almost any profession new media have become widely accepted. Pupils and students should get to now these media in education to prepare them for whatever future career. In the third place new media can support different learning styles and thus can help teachers do justice to those different learning styles. Of course this only works when the new media are used in a proper and sophisticated way. But when that is the case, they can be a powerful tool to deal with differences between different pupils and students in one group.

For what then can new media be used? In the first place new media can serve a role as information and instruction sources. Websites and CD-ROMs can be used to offer information in a way that is normally difficult or even impossible in more classic media. In particular the opportunities for interactive information presentation can be a substantial improvement compared to these classic media. Secondly, new media can be used for performing functions in the process of design and project work that classic media can not fulfill, such as simulation, modeling and animation. An obvious example in teaching about technology is Computer Aided Design (which, by the way, in many cases is not much more than Computer Aided Drawing). But also the simulation of automatic production processes can be mentioned in this respect. In the third place new media can serve a function as communication means. E-mail, for instance, can be used to enrich design experiences in project work. A fourth function is the use of new media in assessing the outcomes of teaching and learning processes.

In the early years of the introduction of new media in education, some mistakes were made that have taught us lessons about how not to go about with new media in education. It is important to make explicit what these lessons were so that we do not keep falling time and again the same pitfalls. A first pitfall lies in the almost addictive nature of the new media. This even became a social problem. People are being treated by psychiatrists for being addicted to web surfing, computer games, and other catching computer facilities. In education the teacher will usually be able to prevent that. Here the danger is different. The teacher might loose sight of the fact that the new media were never meant to be an aim in them selves but always to be a means for achieving educational purposes. Sometimes the new media do become aims in themselves, and this of course should be avoided. In the third place a lack of experience at the teachers' side can cause bad use of the new media or in some cases even causes the new computers to be left packed and stored away. A third problem is that the availability of resources for new media sometimes is certainly not abundant (and this is an understatement). Good hardware and software, suitable for use in education, in some cases lacks. Fourthly there is a lack of standardization that hampers the diffusion of new media in education. It seems to be an ever-recurring problem. Different standards for video recording, for web browsers, in software languages, it all caused headaches for the users of new media.

How then can new media be used in such a way that they help us achieve the purposes that we want to use them for? A first strategy is to let research and development go hand in hand. Good educational research at an early stage of adoption can yield useful insights into what works and what does not work properly. The conference papers have several good examples of such a practice. A second strategy is to be strict in selecting only those new media that really serve our needs. In teaching about technology we teach critical consumership. Here is our chance of showing what that means in practice. We do not want to absorb any new gadget that is presented to us, but first we want to critically review its possible merits and dangers. In a number of cases traditional media are preferable to serve our needs and in those cases the unnecessary use of new media should not be stimulated. Thirdly, we have to be aware of the skills that we loose when new media replace traditional media. Making a technical drawing on paper requires different skills than making it with a CAD program. Perhaps we want our pupils to use the CAD program but still we acknowledge the value of skills that are excluded by that choice. In those cases we have to reflect on how to compensate for that. Perhaps additional assignments need to be designed in order to let pupils and students acquire those 'lost' skills. Of course the (re-) training of teachers was another important strategy that was mentioned. This fourth strategy implies that in training and retraining programs for (future) teachers' critical reflection on the use of technology and the acquisition of certain skills in using them properly should be an integral part. Only then we can hope that teachers will be able to redesign their lessons in such a way the new media are given a useful place. Fifthly and finally, it is important that the use of new media is carefully integrated into the whole process of teaching and learning. The isolated use by pupils of a CD-ROM about whatever topic can hardly be expected to be effective. A holistic perspective is needed to ensure that the new media make the right contribution.

3.   SUPPORT BY EDUCATIONAL RESEARCH

In Chapter 7 some results of educational results have been discussed in order to show that young people often have a narrow view on technology. Evidently, there are educational research studies available as resources of such information. But at the same time it must be admitted that the research support for teaching about technology is still fairly weak. That can be seen when we compare the situation in teaching about technology with the situation in teaching about science. Here a much richer tradition in educational research exists, from which science educators can draw to develop programs that aim at proper conceptualization. For numerous scientific domains, such as mechanics, optics, and electricity, we have a fairly well develop idea of how intuitive concepts are shaped in pupils' minds and how they can be influenced by education. For technology, this is not the case. Even for such basic concepts as systems, we do not have any information about pupils' intuitive concepts, as has been stated already in Chapter 7. The philosophy of technology can be used to develop a research agenda for educational research. Each of the four main aspects of technology, namely technology as artifacts, as knowledge, as processes, and as part of our human nature brings about a set of questions for educational research:

- How do pupils perceive technological *artifacts*? Do they recognize their physical nature? Do they recognize their functional nature?
- Do pupils realize that technological *knowledge* has an inherent normative component? Do they realize that it has a visual component? Are they aware of the knowing-that and the knowing-how types of technological knowledge?
- Do pupils have a clear view of what are essential components of a design *process*? Do they know what is involved in the making of artifacts? Do they realize that the use of technological products can be accompanied by critical evaluation of these products?
- Are pupils aware of the *human* and *social* aspects of technology? Do they recognize both the positive and the negative possible impacts of technology? Are they aware of the non-neutral character of technology or do they have an instrumental view on it?

For each of the aspects the list of questions can easily be extended.

Another way of setting up a research agenda for educational research to support teaching about technology focuses on the difference between the experts' perception of technology and the learners' perception. In this book we have more or less followed that principle. Chapters 2 through 6 presented the experts' vision of technology, Chapter 7 dealt with the learners' concept of technology, and Chapters 8 and 9 discussed ways in which the learners' concept of technology can be influenced to make it more in line with the experts' ideas. A research agenda for teaching about technology based on this approach would look like this:

What do philosophers, engineers, scientists, and other experts claim technology to be? This can be seen as the aims and goals of education;

What do young people and adults (and teachers) think technology is? This can be called the initial situation in education;

How can educational situations be set up that influence the learners' concept of technology so that it gets closer to the experts' opinion? This can be called the educational strategies and settings. The use of media can also be seen as an element in this part of the research agenda.

Although some good research work has been done already, and outcomes are shared in journals such as the International Journal of Technology and Design Education (Kluwer Academic Publishers), the Journal of Technology Education (Virginia Tech and the International Technology Education Association) and the Journal of Technology Studies (the fraternity Epsilon Pi Tau), there is still a long way to go. Hopefully this book can contribute to the further development of teaching about technology at the various levels of education. Technology is an important formative element of our contemporary society. That makes it very worthwhile to work towards a population, whether professionally involved in it or not, that has a correct understanding of its nature. Taking into account the ideas that are and have been developed in the philosophy of technology can certainly be a valuable input in that respect. Besides that, the philosophy is a new and challenging field, of which the study is not only relevant for teaching about technology, but also intriguing in its own right.

Chapter 10

QUESTIONS AND ASSIGNMENTS

For each of the previous Chapters in this book some questions and assignments are offered in this Chapter. The purpose of the questions is to help the reader to produce for him/herself a survey of the main ideas in the Chapter. The questions have been posed in such a way that the list of answers presents an overview of the Chapter. The purpose of the assignments (one per Chapter) is to stimulate the reader to apply the main ideas of the Chapter to new situations, and also to see how these ideas can be used in educational practice.

1.   FOR CHAPTER 1

1.1   Questions

1. Which are the two main functions of philosophy?
2. Which are the five main subfields in philosophy? What do they deal with?
3. What is the role of logic in philosophy?
4. Which two different types of philosophies of technology can be found? What is the difference between them?
5. Which four ways of conceptualizing technology can be found?
6. For which reasons should people which teach about technology get acquainted with the basics of the philosophy of technology?

1.2   Assignment

Try to find a video or DVD that introduces the new field of *nanotechnology*. Try particularly to find one that pays explicit attention to the following aspects of nanotechnology:

- the problems of seeing and manipulating objects at a nanoscale;
- the latest laboratory researches of which it is sometimes not even clear if they will lead to industrial applications;
- nanoapplications in medicine and biotechnology;
- the interdisciplinary character of nanotechnology.

An example of a video/DVD that has all of these aspects is titled 'Nanotechnology' and was produced for the European Commissions (it was and perhaps still is available at no cost). Watch the video/DVD and try to identify what issues are related to this new field in terms of:

- ontology (what is the nature of a nanoartifact?)
- epistemology (what different types of knowledge are involved in nanotechnology?);
- methodology (for example, what is the relationship between research and development in this particular field?);
- metaphysics and teleology (what is the kind of blessings that are promised by the nanotechnology's guru's?)
- ethics (what kind of ethical issues can be found in this new technological field?).

Once you have answered these questions for yourself, now design a classroom activity in which you use the same video/DVD to make pupils and students recognize why this new technology is to intriguing because of the kind of (philosophical) questions that are related to it. Be aware that helping pupils and students raise the right questions is often more important than providing the correct answers!

2.   FOR CHAPTER 2

2.1   Questions

1. Which four types of objects can be distinguished? What is the difference between those types?

2. What meaning can one ascribe to the concept of functions?
3. What is the difference between proper and accidental functions?
4. What is a design plan and what is a user plan?
5. What is collective intentionality and how can it be related to the functions of artifacts?
6. What is meant by the 'dual nature' of technological artifacts?
7. What are differences between conceptualizing functions in biology and in technology?
8. What is a qualifying function? What is a founding function? What do the terms 'subject function' and 'object function' mean? How can these types of functions be used to get to know the nature of an artifact?
9. In what terms can artifacts as systems be conceptualized?

2.2   Assignment

Try to find a book that describes the history of *photocopiers*. Read it and try to identify how each (of perhaps most) of the fifteen aspects as defined by Dooyeweerd, have posed particular problems and challenges for the development of photocopiers. Think for example of the following issues:

- a photocopier has to make a number of copies (arithmetical aspects). In the development of photocopiers no doubt the race for more and more copies in less time was an important issue;
- a photocopier takes room in an office (spatial aspect). No doubt the race for smaller and smaller copiers was an issue also;
- a photocopier now has less moving parts than before (kinematical aspect). Why?
- a photocopier is used by living creatures (biotic aspect) and therefore the emissions of the machine while making copies has been another concern for the designers;
- photocopiers produce signals that can seen, heard and smelled by people (sensitive aspect). How much is acceptable? Another designers' headache;
- the development of photocopiers has been a process in which one type logically follows the next (historical aspect). What line of development can be traced?
- photocopiers are there to enable groups of people to share information on paper (social aspect). How was that aspect taken into account?
- photocopiers cost money and so do copies. Was there also a race for cheaper and cheaper copiers and copies?

- the need for copies that look nice and therefore invite to read (esthetical aspect) no doubt also played a part in the development of copiers. What part?
- as usual the issue of patents is important. What were important patents in the case of photocopiers?
- an ethical aspect in the development of photocopiers is, or at least could have been, the issue of copyrights. How was that dealt with, or was it perhaps neglected?
- to what extent did the belief in the promises of photocopiers drive engineers to keep working on this type of machine?

After you have answered this sort of questions for yourself, now design a classroom activity in which you use the example of the photocopier to make pupils aware of the complexity of real-life design problems.

3.   FOR CHAPTER 3

3.1   Questions

1. What is a 'standard' definition of technology and what critiques on it can be raised by considering technological knowledge?
2. Which types of technological knowledge are identified by Walther Vincenti?
3. Which types of knowledge can be derived from the dual nature of technical artifacts?
4. What characterizes engineering sciences and makes them different from other types of sciences?
5. What are the main approaches in the philosophy of science and how do they describe the growth of knowledge in sciences?
6. Which types of models are used in (engineering) sciences?
7. Which types of analogies are used in engineering sciences?
8. Which levels of interdisciplinarity can be distinguished?

3.2   Assignment

Take a textbook chapter, module, theme or whatever unit of curriculum you will teach in the, not too far away, future. Make an analysis of the different types of knowledge that you will teach in this unit: what propositional knowledge (knowing-that) is in it, what knowing-how, and what visually expressed kind of knowledge. Also identify where you can find clear normative elements in the various types of knowledge that you will teach. For each of the issues on your list, add the educational approach that you planned for teaching that issue. Now critically inspect for each of the issues whether or not the planned approach is in agreement with the type of knowledge. For instance, knowing-how probably is not learnt well by listening to a description of an activity only. What would be a better approach? Also pay attention to the question whether or not your approach does justice to normative elements. Does it become clear that we are not dealing with unchangeable data here, but with norms that result from decisions? How is that reflected in your teaching?

4.   FOR CHAPTER 4

4.1   Questions

1. Which are the three main types of processes in technology?
2. In which four phases can the development of design methodology be described?
3. What is Total Quality Management and what are some of the TQM methods?
4. Which types of technology can be distinguished when focusing on the influences of scientific, technological and social factors on the development of those technologies?
5. What are the main elements in design plans and user plans?
6. What are the differences between production by hand, by machine and by automation?

4.2   Assignment

On the Internet collect information on how the following products were developed: lenses (for glasses, microscopes and telescopes), steam engines, and integrated circuits. For each of these try to find information about the role of scientific, technological, market, political, and juridical aspects. Based on that information, characterize each of these technologies as either an experience-based technology, or a macrotechnology, or a microtechnology. Now design a classroom activity in which the primary aim is to make learners aware of the fact that technologies can be quite different in their development, and that for that reason differentiations (like the one with the three mentioned types of technologies) are necessary for a good understanding of the nature of the various technologies.

5.   FOR CHAPTER 5

5.1   Questions

1. Which levels of human needs can be distinguished?
2. How can artifacts be seen as extensions of human bodies?
3. What types of relationships between humans, technologies and the lifeworld can be distinguished?
4. What is Borgmann's device paradigm?
5. What are limitations of AI and Internet as technology-mediated experiences of the lifeworld?
6. What concerns does cybernetics raise?
7. What expectations do philosophers such as Andrew Feenberg and Langdon Winner have of the possibilities to influence technological developments by politics?
8. What is the view of social constructivists on technology?
9. What is the view of postmodernists on technology?
10. What ways are there to develop lifestyles that resist dominance of technology over one's life?
11. What philosophical mainstreams can be recognized in the whole variety of contemporary philosophers of technology?

5.2   Assignment

Let's make a philosophical analysis of a device that we probably all use daily: the mobile phone. Using the Internet, collect some information on the way it was introduced in our society, and also the effects it appears to have on people. Now see for yourself to what extent you can agree with claims that various philosophers would make about the device:

*   Kapp would see the mobile phone as an extension of the human body;
*   Heidegger would say that the device supports the reduced way of experiencing reality as if it were just resource;
*   Ellul would emphasize the role the mobile phone plays in the systems character of technology that causes us to feel dominated by technology;
*   Borgmann would state that the device causes disengagement in our relation with reality;
*   Feenberg and Winner would point out that the emergence of the mobile phone should have been the result of a balanced influence of engineers and politicians, but probably was not;

- The social constructivists would claim that the mobile phone is just the result of a social process and that technical aspects did not determine the outcome;
- Postmodernists will welcome the mobile phone as another means for doing away with the idea of 'eternal truths' and fixed boundaries.

Now design a classroom activity in which learners are stimulated to reflect on the way the mobile phone influences our life and lifeworld. Try to make it not a purely theoretical project, but one that includes some practical activities also.

6.   FOR CHAPTER 6

6.1   Questions

1. What are some of the famous examples of moral dilemmas in technology?
2. What can be a proper role of logic in ethics?
3. What is meant by deduction, modus ponens, modus tollens, induction, and the naturalistic fallacy.
4. What are the three main approaches in ethics? How can they be recognized in engineering ethics?
5. In what respect can moral problems be treated as if they were design problems?
6. What are the difficulties of dealing with risks?
7. What are the difficulties that result from collective responsibility in technology?
8. In which ways can aesthetical values be expressed in buildings?

6.2   Assignment

Read the story of the accident with the Union Carbide plant in Bhopal, India, in 1984. You will have no problems finding information on the Internet, as it has become a classic case for engineering ethics courses, just like the ones that have been mentioned already in Chapter 6. Now make the following analysis:

- who were the parties involved and what were their interests?
- what was the moral dilemma in this particular case and who was faced with it?

- analyze the moral dilemma by stating all the premises and conclusions, as was done in Chapter 6, thereby carefully distinguishing between facts and norms;
- how did that person/party solve the dilemma (what decision was taken and on what grounds)?
- evaluate that decision: do you think it was based on proper reasoning or not?

Now design a classroom activity in which learners can acquire skills in analyzing moral dilemmas. For higher levels of education the Bhopal case as such can be suitable. Think of a simpler case that can be used for lower levels of education (try to think of something that directly relates to daily experience).

7.   FOR CHAPTER 7

7.1   Questions

1. What are some of the characteristics of pupils' and students' perception of technology?
2. What are some of the characteristics of pupils' and students' attitudes towards technology?
3. What are some of the characteristics of the general public's perception of technology?
4. In what respect can learning about technology be seen as the reconstruction of mental concepts?

7.2   Assignment

Select a number of people, both young people and adult, and conduct *interviews* with them to find out about their concepts of and attitudes towards technology. Think carefully beforehand about the questions that you want to ask them. Make sure you get a good understanding of what they mean by technology in order to understand their attitudes. For younger children you can have them make drawings as a tool for exploring their concepts of technology and people involved in technology. Compare the results with the information that was given in Chapter 7. If there are major differences between your experiences and what you read in Chapter 7, can those be accounted for by taking into account the background of the interviewees?

8. FOR CHAPTER 8

8.1 Questions

1. What are some of the differences and communalities between curricula for teaching about technology in the United States, England and Wales, and Australia?
2. What can be the role of historical case studies in teaching about technology?
3. What can be the role of contemporary case studies in teaching about technology?
4. What is concept mapping and how can it be used in teaching about technology?

8.2 Assignment

Seek out how the concept of *systems* functions in various formal (national) curricula for teaching about technology at the lower secondary level in at least three different countries (including your own country). In most cases you will find a full description of the curricula on the Internet. Compare the differences in functioning of this concept: is it an isolated topic in the curriculum, or is it used as a curricular organizer to arrange parts of the curriculum, or does it have another function?

9. FOR CHAPTER 9

9.1 Questions

1. Which can be the four phases in a continuous line of learning about technology?
2. What can be the role of media in teaching about technology?
3. What can be the impact of educational research on teaching about technology?

9.2 Assignment

Set up a description of how one could teach and learn the concept of *optimization in technology* in the course of the educational path that most people go through (primary, secondary, tertiary), thereby paying particular attention to the gradual progress that can be made by creating a continuous learning line for this concept. Include in the description the use of different types of media (what type of media with what type of content would you select for which phase in the learning line?).

Chapter 11

RESOURCES FOR FURTHER READING AND THINKING
An annotated bibliography

In this final chapter a number of books and other resources will be briefly described. The books have been selected mainly for the following reason: they are well accessible for an audience of people who have no professional background in philosophy, yet are interested to get to know the basic ideas of the philosophy of technology or of general philosophy as a background. When this book was published, all titles were still in print.

1.   BOOKS

1.1   General Philosophy (introductions)

John Hospers, *An introduction to philosophical analysis*. London: Prentice Hall, 1996 (4th edition). 282 pages. ISBN 0-13266305-8.
This book has received wide acclaim for its clarity in introducing philosophical analysis. It deals with the issues of meaning and definition, knowledge, truth, cause, determinism and freedom, metaphysics, philosophy of religion, and ethics in a philosophically very sound way, yet written in such a way that non-philosophers in principle should be able to understand it, although probably not without some serious effort.

Tom Morris, *Philosophy for dummies*. New York: Wiley Publishing, Inc., 1999. 362 pages. ISBN 0-7645-5153-1.

"For dummies" is a series of Wiley books that offer an accessible orientation on a certain field of study. The series is still growing and has volumes on a wide variety of topics and disciplines.

Morris is well aware of the possible negative associations that people may have with philosophy, and he addressed those explicitly in the beginning of the book (some of his quotations have been taken over in Chapter 1 of 'Teaching about Technology"). The book has nine parts, each of them with three chapters (except for the last one, which has only two chapters). Part I introduces the usefulness of philosophy as a professional activity, but also as an activity that every person may get involved in. Part II is about beliefs and knowledge (epistemology), Part III is about ethics ("What is the Good?"), Part IV discusses the issue of human freedom, Part V is about philosophical anthropology (issues like: what is a person, how do body and mind relate?), Part VI is about death and Morris uses this as an entrance for discussing teleological issues. Philosophical reflections on worldviews and religions are the issue of Part VII, while Part VIII brings readers to the heart of teleology: reflections on the meaning of life. Part IX then discusses some famous philosophers and their ideas. Morris does not hide his Christian position but he presents the philosophical debates in a balanced way that does justice to other positions as well. The book throughout has illustrative quotes and stories, which give to the book a very light touch. This, however, does no harm to the quality of the way philosophical issues are introduced.

Gilbert Ryle, *The concept of mind*. Chicago: University of Chicago Press, 1984 (reprint). 348 pages. ISBN 0-22673295-9.

Although not specifically about technology, this philosophical book is well worth reading for those who want to know more about the difference between knowing-that and knowing-how. The latter is an essential component of technological knowledge, and for that reason the book has implications for the philosophy of technology (and is often quoted in that field). Some aptitude for philosophy certainly helps to read this book.

Roger Scruton, *Modern Philosophy. An Introduction and Survey*. New York: Penguin Books, 1996. 612 pages. ISBN 0-14-024907-9.

This book is a good introduction to all the main themes in contemporary (analytical) philosophy. All subdomains of philosophy are addressed: metaphysics, epistemology, ethics, aesthetics, philosophy of science, philosophy of mind, Scruton takes the reader through all of those in a way that is accessible to non-philosophers that are willing to make a certain effort to get a basic understanding of modern philosophy. Scruton is a sort of storyteller: rather than dealing with the various subdomains systematically, he takes the reader from one issue to the next and thus gradually covers all of them. The reader gets to know all the better known names of contemporary (analytical) philosophers and their ideas.

1.2   Philosophy of technology

Davis Baird, *Thing knowledge*. Chicago: Chicago University Press, 2004. 295 pages. ISBN 0-520-23249-6.

Baird contributes to the epistemology of technology by asking attention for the fact that technology is about things, and not about phenomena, as is the case in science. According to him the 'thing-y-ness' of things has often been neglected in the philosophy of technology, in which the focus was often more on the immaterial aspects of technology, that is, on ideas rather than on things. In particular instrumentation is a topic that Baird uses frequently to make his point.

Ian G. Barbour, *Ethics in an age of technology*. San Francisco: Harper & Row, 1993. 312 pages. ISBN 0-06060934-6.

This book contains a series of lectures and offers a good survey of the variety of ethical issues that can be found in technology.

Albert Borgmann, *Technology and the character of contemporary life: a philosophical inquiry*. Chicago: University of Chicago Press, 1984. 302 pages. ISBN 0-226-06628-2.

Albert Borgmann, *Crossing the postmodern divide*. London: University of Chicago Press, 1992. 173 pages. ISBN 0-226066-27-4.

Eric Higgs, Andrew Light and David Strong, *Technology and the good life?* Chicago: University of Chicago Press. 392 pages. ISBN 0-226-33386-8.

Borgmann is one the better known philosophers of technology. He is best known for his 'device paradigm', in which he expressed the idea that devices have been put between ourselves and our lifeworld, so that we experience that lifeworld not as rich as it is. Borgmann makes a play for 'focal activities' that enable us to gave rich experiences with the lifeworld (like jogging). Borgmann has also sketched the postmodern features of various contemporary technologies, such as architecture and internet. The Higgs/Light/Strong book contains responses of other philosophers to Borgmann's ideas.

Louis L. Bucciarelli, *Designing engineers*. Cambridge: MIT Press, 1994. 220 pages. ISBN 0-262-02377-6

In this book, Bucciarelli offers a number of elaborate case studies, through which he shows how design processes are not just a matter of technical aspects, but also of social interactions. X-ray inspection systems at airports, photoprint machines, and a residential energy system serve as examples of how engineering design is a socially-defined process. Through case studies readers are shown how business and management issues as engineering design influence the conceptualization and production of technology.

Subrata Dasgupta, Technology and creativity. Oxford: Oxford University Press, 1996. 233 pages. ISBN 0-19-509688-6.

In this book Dasgupta offers a survey of various philosophical perspectives on technological developments and in particular the role of creativity and knowledge in that.

Randall R. Dipert, *Artifacts, Art Works and Agency*. Philadelphia: Temple University Press, 1993. pages. ISBN

A book that offers one of the first philosophical analyses of what we mean by technical artifacts, as they differ from other types of artifacts and of natural objects.

Hubert L. Dreyfus, *What computers still can't do. A critique of artificial reason.* Cambridge: MIT Press, 1992. 354 pages. ISBN 0-262-54067-3.

Hubert L. Dreyfus, *On the Internet*. London/New York: Routledge, 2001. 127 pages. ISBN 0-415-22807-7.

These are two books that criticize the high expectations many people have of artificial intelligence and of the Internet. Dreyfus emphasizes that humans have characteristics that are essential and can not be replaced by technology.

Jacques Ellul, *The technological bluff* (transl. Geoffrey W. Bromiley). Grand Rapids: Eerdmans, 1990. 418 pages. ISBN 0-8028-3678-X

This is an English translation of the original French book. Ellul present a very pessimistic view on technology. According to him, technology has become an almost entirely autonomous system, against which humans can do nothing but try to make the best of it. Although there are few people now who still agree totally with Ellul's dark picture of technology, his ideas are still worth reading for those who are interested in dystopian view on technology. After all, Ellul is still cited often as a 'classic' in the philosophy of technology.

Andrew Feenberg, *Alternative modernity: the technical turn in philosophy and social theory*. London: University of California Press, 1995. 251 pages. ISBN 0-520-08986-3.

Andrew Feenberg, *Questioning Technology*. London: Routledge, 1999. 243 pages. ISBN 0-415-19755-4.

Feenberg is a contemporary often cited philosopher of technology and his books are pretty well accessible for interested non-philosophers. Feenberg, like Winner, brings to the fore the notion that technological developments are not autonomous, but can be changed by the public opinion. The example he describes is the French Minitel system, of which the main function changed dramatically under the influence of public use.

Eugene S. Ferguson, *Engineering and the Mind's Eye*. Cambridge, MA: MIT Press, 1992. 242 pages. ISBN 0-262-06147-3.

Ferguson makes a contribution to the philosophy of technology by pointing out that a special feature of engineers' knowledge is: a visual component. Part of what engineers know can only be represented adequately in pictures, sketches, drawings and the like. Ferguson in the end criticizes the education of engineers in that it has focused too much on the written component and has moved away from this indispensable visual component. In the book Ferguson presents a well-illustrated survey of the variety of visualization tools that engineers have at their disposal when designing and communicating about designs.

Frederick Ferré, *Philosophy of Technology*. Englewood Cliffs, NJ: Prentice Hall, 1988. 148 pages. ISBN 0-13-662586-X.

Ferré's book is an introduction to the philosophy of technology in which both analytical parts and critical parts can be found. The author uses epistemology (reflection on knowledge), axiology (reflection on values), metaphysics (reflection on reality) and methodology (reflection on processes) as the main fields in the philosophy of technology).

Charles E. Harris, Michael S. Pritchard and Michael J. Rabins, *Engineering Ethics. Concepts and cases*. Belmont, CA: Wadsworth, 2000. 377 pages. ISBN 0-534-53397-3.

Although this book is primarily meant for engineering students, it is well readable for technology educators too. The authors present a sort of standard approach to engineering ethics and the book is fairly representative of other books with similar titles. Such books cover issues like: reasoning in moral dilemmas, various ethical approaches (utilitarian, deontic, virtues), responsibility, integrity, reliability, risks, safety, environmental issues, and professional ethical codes. The book goes with a CD-ROM that contains a number of case studies that can be used to explore these concepts in practical examples.

Larry Hickman, *Philosophical Tools for Technological Culture*. Bloomington and Indianapolis: Indiana University Press, 2001. 201 pages. ISBN 0-253-33869-7

This book offers a philosophy of technology that is inspired by John Dewey's pragmatist approach. It contains a collection of separate articles. In line with Dewey's philosophy Hickman conceptualizes technology in terms of a creative problem solving process. A possible critique is that he defines technology in such a wide way that all problem-solving activities can be called 'technology'.

Don Ihde, *Technics and praxis*. Dordrecht: Reidel, 1979. 151 pages. ISBN 90-277-0953-X

Don Ihde, *Technology and the lifeworld: from garden to earth*. Bloomington: Indiana University Press, 1990. 226 pages. ISBN 0-253-32900-0

In both books Ihde points out that one of the characteristics of technology is that it intermediates between us and our lifeworld in that it often shapes the way we experience things. Ihde is a phenomenologist and often uses Heidegger's ideas to describe the way technology influences our lives. Sometimes the technology almost becomes part of ourselves when we observe the word (e.g. in the case of contact lenses), sometimes it becomes part of the lifeworld that we observe as something outside ourselves.

Peter Kroes and Anthonie Meijers (eds.), *The Empirical Turn in the Philosophy of Technology*. Oxford: Elsevier Science, 2000. 258 pages. ISBN 0-7623-0755-2.

This book contains a collection of articles that show how the philosophy of technology can be empirically informed. That is not the same as to make philosophy into an empirical science as happens in the 'sociological' turn in the philosophy of technology, whereby the character of philosophy almost totally is hidden behind the characteristics of sociology. In the Kroes and Meijers book philosophy remains philosophy. Yet, the philosophical reflections in this book are inspired by empirical studies, either done by the philosophers themselves or, perhaps even preferably, by others (historians, sociologists, etcetera). The contributions deal with ontology of artifacts, the nature of technological knowledge (epistemology) and engineering ethics.

Carl Mitcham, *Thinking Through Technology*. Chicago: University of Chicago Press, 1994. 398 pages. ISBN 0-226-53198-8.

Mitcham's book is almost like a 'classic' in the philosophy of technology as an introduction to its main topics and an account of its historical development. This book has been an important model for determining the structure of "Teaching about Technology". The first part of the book is mainly historical and introduces the two types of philosophy of technology: the Continental, or cultural one, which Mitcham indicates by: "humanities philosophy of technology". Furthermore there is the more analytical one, which Mitcham calls "engineering philosophy of technology". The second part of the book is mainly systematic in nature and introduces the four main ways of conceptualizing technology: as objects, actions, knowledge and volition. For each of those four Mitcham presents the main ideas that have been brought to the forum by various philosophers, both in the continental and in the analytical strand. A substantial part of the 'actions' chapter is dedicated to design, and Mitcham presents a nice survey of developments in design methodology here, thereby drawing from previous surveys such as the one that was edited by De Vries in the NATO ASI Series.

Lewis Mumford, *Technics and civilization*. San Diego: Harcourt Brace Jovanovich, 1963. 495 pages. ISBN 0-15-688254-X.
Lewis Mumford, *The myth of the machine*. San Diego: Harcourt Brace Jovanovich, 1967-1970 (2 volumes). 342+496 pages. ISBN 0-15-662341-2 and ISBN 0-15-163974-4.
Mumford is a 'classic' read in the philosophy of technology. These are just two of his books. Together they give a good impression of his writings. It is very good in placing technological developments in their social and cultural context.

David Noble, *The religion of technology: the divinity of man and the spirit of invention*. New York: Penguin Books, 1999. 273 pages. ISBN 0-14-027916-4.
In this book Noble shows that in the course of time the expectations that were raised by technology were in a certain sense of a religious nature. Technology was to bring salvation and redemption, the restoring of the original perfection of creation. Consequently, a critical attitude towards technology can be repressed because of this 'belief' in technology, and this is what Noble wants to warn for.

Joseph Pitt, *Thinking about Technology*. London: Seven Bridges Press, 2000. 146 pages. ISBN 1-889119-12-1.
In this book Pitt offers a survey of philosophical issues related to philosophy. In particular he discusses differences between science and technology. He starts by putting technology in the perspective of practical

reasoning and rationality. Then he deals with the question of what makes engineering knowledge different from scientific knowledge. Next he compares scientific and technological explanations. Part of the book is devoted to issues of ideologies, values, democracy, and autonomy of technology versus control over technology. Finally Pitt describes the technological infrastructure of science.

Friedrich Rapp, *Analytical philosophy of technology*. Dordrecht: Reidel, 1981. 199 pages. ISBN 90-277-1222-0.

As the title indicates, Rapp wants to offer a philosophy of technology in the analytical rather than the Continental tradition (although he is from the Continent, geographically speaking). Rapp in this book deals with such issues as how the nature of technology has changed through time (from traditional to modern), how technology can be seen as a transformation of the material world, how technology is a human activity that has not only technical, but also socio-economic aspects. The author also discusses the tension between freedom and control in the role of technology in society.

Robert C. Scharff (ed.), *Philosophy of technology: the technological condition. An Anthology*. Blackwell Publishers, 2002. 600 pages. ISBN 0-63122219-7.

This book contains a collection of more or less 'classical' articles in the philosophy of technology. The book is pretty much biased towards the Continental strand and not much analytical articles can be found in it (although the difference becomes blurred nowadays). Part I goes back as far as Plato and Aristotle, Part II is about positivist and post-positivist philosophies of science (there is four articles on technology at the end of this part), Part III, called 'Defining technology' in fact deals with the social constructivist view on technology, Part IV is on Heidegger and followers (e.g. Ihde, Borgmann), Part V deals with human beings as tool makers (articles by a.o. Lewis Mumford, Jacques Ellul and Hannah Ahrend and a section on ecology), Part VI has the lifeworld, cyberspace and knowledge as sub-themes (articles by a.o. Dreyfus, Foucault, Feenberg and Winner). An excellent start for those who want to read the original articles by a number of the important continentally-oriented philosophers of technology.

Egbert Schuurman, *Perspectives on technology and culture*. Potchefstroom: Institute for Reformational Studies, 1997. 164 pages. ISBN 1-86822-194-6.

Schuurman offers a concise introduction to the philosophy of technology is this book. He discusses differences between traditional and modern technologies, the conflict between freedom and control, ethics of technology and the main ground motives for technology (here he draws from Dooyeweerd, a Dutch philosopher), and in particular a Christian perspective on technology.

Kristin Shrader-Frechette and Laura Westra (Eds.), *Technology and values*. Lanham, MD: Rowman & Littelfield Publishers, Inc., 1997. 472 pages. ISBN 0-8476-8631-0.

This book is a collection of articles on values in technology. The issue of morality and ethics is introduced in the first part (three articles), then alternative views of technology (resulting in different values) are presented in the second part (seven articles), strategies for evaluating values in technology are the focus of the third part (five papers) and a set of case studies (nine articles) conclude the book.

Herbert A. Simon, *The sciences of the artificial*. Cambridge, MA: MIT Press. 231 pages. ISBN 0-262-69191-4.

Simon's book counts as a 'classic' for philosophy of technology. It must be read against the background of its time, when cybernetics was very much increasing in popularity. Nevertheless, it still contains interesting reflections for today.

Caroline Whitbeck, *Ethics in Engineering Practice and research*. Cambridge: Cambridge University Press, 1998. 330 pages. ISBN 0-521-47944-4.

Whitbeck's book on engineering ethics is different from most other books in the same field in that is sees moral problems as a specific case of design problems. This contrasts the idea that most author present in which engineering ethics is a matter of choosing the best (or less problematic) solution in a moral dilemma. Whitbeck shows that it is possible, and often preferable, to seek new, creative solution for such problems. Although meant for engineering students, the book is certainly accessible to non-specialists.

1.3   History and sociology of technology (as an empirical source of inspiration for philosophy of technology)

George Basalla, *The evolution of technology*. Cambridge: Cambridge University Press, 1988. 248 pages. ISBN 0-521-29681-1

Basalla described the development of technology as an evolutionary process. New variants of devices came into existence and through a 'survival of the fittest' selection process the best designs remained. Although Basalla uses many examples to underpin his ideas, several historians and philosophers think his perception of technological developments is certainly not correct for all such developments.

Wybe E. Bijker, *Of bicycles, bakelites and bulbs: towards a theory of sociotechnical change*. London: MIT Press, 1995. 380 pages. ISBN 0-262-02376-8

Wijbe E. Bijker and John Law (eds.), *Shaping technology, building society: studies in sociotechnical change*. London: MIT Press, 1992. 341 pages. ISBN 0-262-02338-5

Bijker is one of the leading figures in what is sometimes called the 'sociological turn in the philosophy of technology'. Although his studies do reflect on the nature of technology, the emphasis is so much on the role of social actors that it belongs to sociology more than to philosophy. Together with John Law and others Bijker has given shape to a stream that is generally indicated as SCOT: the social construction of technology. These constructivists claim that technology is primarily shaped by social factors, not by technical factors. Because of their case study oriented approach the SCOT publications read like a novel.

Henry Petroski, *To engineer is human. The role of failure in successful design*. London: McMillan, 1985. 247 pages. ISBN 0-333-40673-7.

Henry Petroski, *The evolution of useful things*. New York: Knopf, 1992. 288 pages. ISBN 0-679-41226-3.

Henry Petroski, *Design paradigms: case studies of error and judgment in engineering*. New York: Cambridge University Press, 1994. 209 pages. ISBN 0-521-46649-0.

Henry Petroski, *Invention by design: how engineers get from thought to thing*. London: Harvard University Press, 1996. 242 pages. ISBN 0-674-46367-6.

Henry Petroski, *Remaking the world: adventures in engineering*. New York: Knopf, 1997. 239 pages. ISBN 0-375-40041-9.

This list is not exhaustive and it shows how successful Henry Petroski has been in publishing all sorts of case studies of technological developments, most of them about well-known, everyday-life inventions. All of his books point out the human aspects in such developments and the fact that this human side of technology can lead to errors in designs. It is healthy to read these books for all those who still have a too heroic image of technology.

Robert Poole, *Beyond Engineering. How Society Shapes Technology*. Oxford, Oxford University Press, 1997. 359 pages. ISBN 0-19-512911-3.

The main message of this book is that social factors play an important part in the development of new technologies. Poole uses examples such as nuclear energy, automobiles, light bulbs, electricity networks and personal computers to illustrate this. The story-telling nature of this book makes it accessible to a wide audience. In particular the role of business interests, complexity, choice making, risk assessment, control over technology and technology management are presented.

Neil Postman, *The surrender of culture to technology*. New York: Knopf, 1992. 222 pages. ISBN 0-394-58272-1.

A critical book about the negative impact technology often has on our culture. In particular the dubious role of television is discussed by Postman.

John M. Staudenmaier, *Technology's storytellers: reweaving the human fabric*. London: MIT Press, 1985. 282 pages. ISBN 0-262-19237-3

This book is a survey of themes that run through the articles that have been published in the Technology & Culture journal for the history of technology. As Staudenmaier offers a great deal of reflection on those themes, this book could almost count as a philosophy book. But its main purpose is to investigate the outcomes of historical research studies, and for that reason it has here been categorized as 'history of technology'. The themes that are identified by Staudenmaier are the following:

Marc J. de Vries, *80 Years of Research at Philips. The History of the Philips Natuurkundig Laboratorium, 1914-1994*. Eindhoven: Foundation for the History of Technology, 2001 (to be published by Amsterdam University Press in 2005).

In this book the history of the main research laboratory of the Philips company is presented. Philips is a multinational electronics company that produces a great variety of electronics products such as video and audio equipment, but also medical imaging equipment and a variety of household apparatuses. This book shows three different ways of operating in its mother company for an industrial research laboratory. In the period 1914-1947 the research lab served as the main organization through which the company could realize its ambitions to extend the product portfolio. In the period 1947-1972 the lab functioned in a much more isolated way (the 'ivory tower' perception that many people may have of such a lab was more or less true for this period). A linear model was used for reaching entirely new products (basic research first, then development-oriented research, followed by development and implementation). In the period 1972-1994 a shift was made towards the delivery of specific knowledge that was demanded by the product divisions. These three periods also reflect three different interaction patterns between science and technology, and therefore serves as a source of inspiration for philosophical reflections on science and technology.

Walther G. Vincenti, *What Engineers Know and How They Know It*. Baltimore: Johns Hopkins Press, 1990. 326 pages. ISBN 0-8018-4588-2.

This book is a good example of how informed historical storytelling can lead to philosophical considerations about technology and the knowledge involved in that. The book is a collection of papers that had previously been published in Technology & Culture, the journal of the Society for the History Of Technology (SHOT). Each of these papers describes an example of aeronautical design and each paper focuses on a particular aspect of the work of the aeronautical engineers working on their aircraft designs. From these case studies Vincenti concludes that at least the following types of engineering knowledge can be distinguished: fundamental design concepts, criteria and specifications, theoretical tools, quantitative data, practical considerations, and design instrumentalities. He also investigated the mechanisms through which engineers gain these types of knowledge and concludes that transfer from science only plays a modest part in that (other sources of engineers' knowledge are: invention, theoretical and experimental engineering research, design practice, production, and direct trial). The book is one of the first in which a serous effort is made to come up with an empirically informed taxonomy of technological knowledge.

Langdon Winner, *Autonomous technology: technics-out-of-control as a theme in political thought*. London: MIT Press, 1977. 386 pages. ISBN 0-262-73049-9.

Langdon Winner, *The whale and the reactor: a search for limits in an age of high technology*. London: University of Chicago Press, 1986. 200 pages, ISBN 0-226-90210-2.

As with other sociological oriented books on technology, it is hard to decide whether one should rank them as 'philosophy of technology' or 'sociology of technology'. Winner very much focuses on the political aspects of technology. He makes clear the tension between technological developments ("the reactor") and preserving our environment ("the wale") and the role politicians have to play in deciding about this rather than leaving decisions to the engineers. Reading his books does not require a background in philosophy.

1.4   Design Methodology

Nigel Cross, *Developments in design methodology*. Chichester: Wiley, 1984. 357 pages. ISBN 0-471-10248-2

Nigel Cross, *Engineering design methods: strategies for product design.* Chichester: Wiley, 2000. 212 pages. ISBN 0-471-87250-4

Two books by a leading design methodologist: one that sketches the general developments of design methodology as a scientific discipline that aims at exploring design processes and methods, the other a textbook on design methods. Cross shows how thinking in design methodology has evolved from a rather naïve towards design prescriptions to a more sophisticated and balanced use of methods for design work. Together the books give a good impression of the theoretical and the practical side of design methodology.

Norbert Roozenburg and Johannes Eekels, *Product design: fundamentals and methods.* Chichester: John Wiley & Sons, 1995. 408 pages. ISBN 0-471-95465-9.

This is a good introductory text to design processes and design methods. The book is based on extensive experience in teaching at an academic engineering program for industrial design.

Donald Schön, *The reflective practitioner: how professionals think in action.* New York: Basic Books, 1983. 374 ISBN 0-465-06876-6.

This book came out in many editions, so the exact bibliographical data differ also (date, publisher). The book deals with the way designers (and other professionals) in the course of time learn to reflect on their own design practice. It contrasts the idea that designers should be guided by standard, rigid methods.

Marc J. de Vries, Nigel Cross and Donald Grant (eds.), *Design methodology and relationships with science.* Dordrecht: Kluwer Academic Publishers, 1993. 327 pages. ISBN 0-7923-2191-X.

This book was the result of a NATO Advanced Research Workshop that has been held in 1992 to bring together experts from philosophy, history and design methodology to see how these fields study design processes in complementary ways. A selection of the presented papers is now available to others to get an impression of the state-of-the-art in research about design processes and methods.

1.5   Cognitive sciences

Donald A. Norman, *The design of everyday things.* London: MIT Press, 1998. 257 pages. ISBN 0-262-64-07-6.

Donald A. Norman, *Turn signals are the facial expressions of automobiles*. Reading, MA: Addison-Wesley, Inc., 1992. 205 pages. ISBN 0-201-58124-8.

Donald A. Norman, *Things that make us smart. Defending human attributes in the age of the machine*. Reading, MA: Addison-Wesley, Inc., 1993. 290 pages. ISBN 0-201-58129-9.

Norman's books are full of everyday life examples of how designers can either help users by shaping the artifacts in such a way that they contain signals about their proper use, or mislead them by lack of such signals. Although Norman's work is not philosophical, it is certainly of philosophical interest to read it because it can give useful input for philosophical reflections on how people perceive artifacts.

1.6   Technology Education Philosophy

Greg Pearson and A. Thomas Young (eds.), *Technically Speaking. Why All Americans Need to Know More About Technology*. Washington, DC: National Academy Press, 2002. 156 pages. ISBN 0-309-08262-5.

This report was the outcome of a National Academy of Engineering committee study into the concept of technological literacy. The report makes extensive use of literature in the field of philosophy of technology. At the same time it described the importance of technological literacy as a part of the intellectual and practical capability of all citizens.

International Technology Education Association, *Standards for Technological Literacy. Content for the Study of Technology*. Reston, VA: ITEA/Technology for All Americans Project. 248 pages. ISBN 1-887101-02-0.

This publication operationalizes technological literacy in terms of 20 standards, divided into five main categories: the nature of technology, technology and society, design, abilities for a technological world, and the designed world (this term is used to indicate the main fields of engineering: medical technology, agricultural technology, energy and power technology, information and communication technology, transportation technology, manufacturing technology and construction technology). The report makes extensive use of literature from the philosophy of technology.

Marc J. de Vries and Arley Tamir, *Shaping concepts of technology: from philosophical perspectives to mental images*. Dordrecht: Kluwer Academic Publishers, 1997. 201 pages. ISBN 0-7923-4647-5.

This book is a collection of articles. In the first part of the book there are philosophical articles (the 'philosophical perspectives') by Paul Gardner,

Joseph Agassi, Günther Ropohl, Klaus Hennig-Hansen and Marc de Vries. In the second part there are articles on education (dealing with the 'mental images' part of the book title) by Alister Jones, Carole Thomson, Ron Hansen, Ann-Marie Hill, Bob McCormick, Scott Johnson and Alain Durey. The combination of the two parts allows readers to see how philosophical debates about technology can have consequences for technology education.

2.   JOURNALS

International Journal of Technology & Design Education

This is an academic journal in the field of technology education, but with regular appearance of articles that refer to philosophical literature. Besides that it has special issues on the philosophy of technology and its consequences for teaching about philosophy. It is published by Kluwer Academic Publishers (now Springer) and available both in hardcopy version as well as electronically.

Techne

This is the name of the electronic journal that is published by the Society for Philosophy of Technology (see below). It is accessible for everyone, but the articles range from introductory to very much in-depth. Yet it is worthwhile to keep track of what is published in it, since many interesting articles have been in it already and available at no cost.

Technology & Culture

Although this journal is primarily about the history of technology, there are also articles with a philosophical element. For example, Vincenti's book on What Engineers Know and How They Know It (see the list of books under History of technology) was published as a series of articles in this journal.

3.   ORGANIZATIONS

Society for Philosophy of Technology

This is an international society that organizes conferences every other year and publishes the electronic journal Techne (see above). The conference sites alternate between the USA and Europe. Papers that are presented differ quite much in accessibility for non-philosophers, but generally speaking one can always find a number of sessions that are worthwhile to attend even without much philosophical background.

Society for the History Of Technology (SHOT)

This society also organizes bi-annual conferences, where papers are presented that often are interesting for those who want to learn about philosophy of technology. The society also published the Technology & Culture journal (see above).

SUBJECT INDEX

161

NAME INDEX

Adorno, T. 78, 84
Agassi, J. 159
Aristotle 94, 152

Baird, D. 38, 147
Barbour, I.G. 147
Basalla, G. 153
Behe, M. 21
Bijker, W. 78, 79, 154
Boden, M. 45, 46
Borgmann, A. 71-73, 83, 84, 140, 147, 152
Bratman, M. 34
Bucciarelli, L.L. 147, 148

Chatoney-Ginestié, M. 111, 113
Cross, N.G. 49, 156, 157
Cummins, R. 20

Dasgupta, S. 148
Davis, R.S. 111, 113
De Vries, M.J. 124, 151, 155, 157-159
Dembski, W. 21
Dennett, D. 21
Dewey, J. 72, 84, 150
Dipert, R.R. 13, 14, 16, 24, 25, 148
Dooyeweerd, H. 2, 23, 36, 45, 60, 61, 137, 153

Science & Technology Education Library

Series editor: William W. Cobern, *Western Michigan University, Kalamazoo, U.S.A.*

Publications
1. W.-M. Roth: *Authentic School Science.* Knowing and Learning in Open-Inquiry Science Laboratories. 1995   ISBN 0-7923-3088-9; Pb: 0-7923-3307-1
2. L.H. Parker, L.J. Rennie and B.J. Fraser (eds.): *Gender, Science and Mathematics.* Shortening the Shadow. 1996   ISBN 0-7923-3535-X; Pb: 0-7923-3582-1
3. W.-M. Roth: *Designing Communities.* 1997
          ISBN 0-7923-4703-X; Pb: 0-7923-4704-8
4. W.W. Cobern (ed.): *Socio-Cultural Perspectives on Science Education.* An International Dialogue. 1998   ISBN 0-7923-4987-3; Pb: 0-7923-4988-1
5. W.F. McComas (ed.): *The Nature of Science in Science Education.* Rationales and Strategies. 1998   ISBN 0-7923-5080-4
6. J. Gess-Newsome and N.C. Lederman (eds.): *Examining Pedagogical Content Knowledge.* The Construct and its Implications for Science Education. 1999
          ISBN 0-7923-5903-8
7. J. Wallace and W. Louden: *Teacher's Learning.* Stories of Science Education. 2000
          ISBN 0-7923-6259-4; Pb: 0-7923-6260-8
8. D. Shorrocks-Taylor and E.W. Jenkins (eds.): *Learning from Others.* International Comparisons in Education. 2000   ISBN 0-7923-6343-4
9. W.W. Cobern: *Everyday Thoughts about Nature.* A Worldview Investigation of Important Concepts Students Use to Make Sense of Nature with Specific Attention to Science. 2000   ISBN 0-7923-6344-2; Pb: 0-7923-6345-0
10. S.K. Abell (ed.): *Science Teacher Education.* An International Perspective. 2000
          ISBN 0-7923-6455-4
11. K.M. Fisher, J.H. Wandersee and D.E. Moody: *Mapping Biology Knowledge.* 2000
          ISBN 0-7923-6575-5
12. B. Bell and B. Cowie: *Formative Assessment and Science Education.* 2001
          ISBN 0-7923-6768-5; Pb: 0-7923-6769-3
13. D.R. Lavoie and W.-M. Roth (eds.): *Models of Science Teacher Preparation.* Theory into Practice. 2001   ISBN 0-7923-7129-1
14. S.M. Stocklmayer, M.M. Gore and C. Bryant (eds.): *Science Communication in Theory and Practice.* 2001   ISBN 1-4020-0130-4; Pb: 1-4020-0131-2
15. V.J. Mayer (ed.): *Global Science Literacy.* 2002   ISBN 1-4020-0514-8
16. D. Psillos and H. Niedderer (eds.): *Teaching and Learning in the Science Laboratory.* 2002   ISBN 1-4020-1018-4
17. J.K. Gilbert, O. De Jong, R. Justi, D.F. Treagust and J.H. Van Driel (eds.): *Chemical Education: Towards Research-based Practice.* 2003   ISBN 1-4020-1112-1
18. A.E. Lawson: *The Neurological Basis of Learning, Development and Discovery.* Implications for Science and Mathematics Instruction. 2003   ISBN 1-4020-1180-6
19. D.L. Zeidler (ed.): *The Role of Moral Reasoning on Socioscientific Issues and Discourse in Scientific Education.* 2003   ISBN 1-4020-1411-2

Science & Technology Education Library

Series editor: William W. Cobern, *Western Michigan University, Kalamazoo, U.S.A.*

20. P.J. Fensham: *Defining an Identity. The Evolution of Science Education as a Field of Research.* 2003 ISBN 1-4020-1467-8
21. D. Geelan: *Weaving Narrative Nets to Capture Classrooms.* Multimethod Qualitative Approaches for Educational Research. 2003
ISBN 1-4020-1776-6; Pb: 1-4020-1468-7
22. A. Zohar: *Higher Order Thinking in Science Classrooms: Students' Learning and Teachers' Professional Development.* 2004
ISBN 1-4020-1852-5; Pb: 1-4020-1853-3
23. C.S. Wallace, B. Hand, V. Prain: *Writing and Learning in the Science Classroom.* 2004 ISBN 1-4020-2017-1
24. I.A. Halloun: *Modeling Theory in Science Education.* 2004 ISBN 1-4020-2139-9
25. L.B. Flick and N.G. Lederman (eds.): *Scientific Inquiry and the Nature of Science.* Implications for Teaching, Learning, and Teacher Education. 2004
ISBN 1-4020-2671-4
26. W.-M. Roth, L. Pozzer-Ardhenghi and J.Y. Han: *Critical Graphicacy.* Understanding Visual Representation Practices in Scholl Science. 2005 ISBN 1-4020-3375-3
27. M.J. de Vries: *Teaching about Technology.* An Introduction to the Philosophy of Technology for Educators. 2005 ISBN 1-4020-3409-1